The Tangled Lamb

Joanna Tinsley with Noel Davidson

THE TANGLED LAMB
© Copyright Noel Davidson November 2013

ISBN 978-1-909751-13-2

Printed by
jcprintltd
BELFAST
Telephone 07860 205333
email: info@jcprint.net

CONTENTS

INTRODUCTION

When God created this world He began with darkness. Shapeless, emptiness. And absolute darkness.

We read that 'the earth was without form, and void; and darkness was upon the face of the deep'.

In the next verse, though, we discover that it was not His plan that it should remain that way. And find that He had the power to make a difference.

'God said, Let there be light, and there was light.'

At the command of God, light dispelled darkness, and fullness replaced emptiness.

That was in the physical world, but the same rule applies in the spiritual realm also.

There are two lines of a hymn which express it so accurately when stating:-

> 'The whole world was lost in the darkness of sin,
>   The Light of the world is Jesus ...'

This book traces the steps and struggles of one person in her transition from darkness to light.

Joanna Maciantowicz was raised in Poland during difficult days, but as she grew older she realised that although her soul seemed enveloped in blackness, there was a light source somewhere. 'The light at the end of the tunnel', was how she imagined it.

Her restless teenage developed into one long search for satisfaction and peace. The light was elusive. Always there, but dim in the distance. Then she met someone who introduced her to the Bible, and who was in daily, vital contact with the Light of the World …

It has been a thrill and a challenge for me to retrace that journey with Joanna. The hopeful signs, and the big let downs, the spiritual battles and the eventual victory…

Joanna is an artist, and the writing of this book was very much like the painting of a picture.

There is a main theme. The passage from darkness into light, from mental misery to spiritual calm, from the ranks of Satan into the family of God.

But there is more to it than that.

Two sub-plots snake their way through the story, adding interest to the picture.

There is the tale of the talented artist, whose ability was discovered in childhood, whose art proved a valuable life-line of expression in turbulent times, and whose gift has been blessed by God.

The second interwoven theme is a remarkable love story. How that God took over Joanna's life in a miraculous way, and in an almost unbelievable manner led her and a young man called Colin, together. Although he was from a distant country and a different culture, Joanna and he were both awestruck to discover that they each shared a common Christian faith. A deeply loving relationship can be hard to maintain, though, a thousand miles apart. There were many thrilling times together and agonising ages apart …

While working on this book it has been the joy, and indeed privilege, of both my wife, Liz, and me, to meet Joanna and Colin, a number of times, both at home and for a few most inspirational and instructive days, in Joanna's beautiful home city of Krakow. On each and every occasion we have met, one can never fail to be impressed with this young couple's fervent zeal to serve the Lord in a meaningful way.

As you read this story it is our prayer that you will experience, in a very real sense, the warmth and light of the love of God. The warmth and light that can dispel the cold and dark of a life lived without Christ.

Finally, you will probably be wondering about the title.

This introduction has been all about persuasive darkness and radiant light, a gifted artist and a wonderful love. And not a word about lambs.

What do you mean by a *tangled* lamb, anyway, you ask?

Sorry, but you are going to have to read on to find out!

And may God richly bless you as you do!

Noel I Davidson
October, 2000

1

RATIONED!

"Wake up, Joanna! Wake up!"

It was just after five o'clock on a Saturday morning in late October, 1980, in the city of Krakow, in southern Poland.

Eleven year-old Joanna was sound asleep but her older brother Thomas seemed to believe that she should be aroused. And soon.

"Wake up, I said, Joanna! Hurry up! Wake up!" he repeated, grabbing his much too sleepy sister by the shoulders and giving her an urgent shake. As she rubbed her eyes and stretched slowly into wakefulness Joanna mumbled, "What is it, Thomas? What now?"

"A car has just arrived at the back of the shop!" Thomas told her excitedly, as she struggled up on to one elbow. "You should get up and join the queue before it becomes too long!"

Food rationing had been introduced in their country, and times were tough.

Essentials were in short supply. Luxuries were rare.

A car at the back of the shop, across the open green recreation area in the front of their flat, then, was a significant signal in that situation. It meant that food of some sort was being delivered. And if food of some sort was being delivered you had to be sure to queue for your ration!

Joanna pushed off the bedclothes, swung around, sat motionless, like a monument, for a moment, on the edge of the bed, and then stood up. She then went into the bathroom, splashed some water over her face, and slid a comb half-heartedly through her fine wispy hair. Very soon she was dressed and had pulled on her only heavy coat.

Not having taken time to eat any of the family's precious store of food, Joanna was ready for out. For off. For into the queue.

There was only one essential item she had to take with her. Everybody in the already-forming line stretching away from the front of the shop would have one, so she had better not forget hers. It was the coarse shopping bag with the strong leather handles, containing the ration-books and a small amount of money. This bag occupied a permanent position on the corner of their small wooden kitchen table, and was always maintained in a high state of readiness. Like a fire extinguisher. Or a rescue-helicopter crew. You were just never sure when you were going to need it!

The heat of summer had long gone from Krakow, and the bracing chill of autumn had almost surrendered to the bitter, biting cold of an approaching Polish winter, when Joanna stepped outside that morning. As she trudged across the field to the shop she could see that the straggling queue was growing steadily. A few people greeted each other in hushed tones, but mostly they just made their way along to the end of the line in silence. And there they stood mostly in silence. The only certain sound to shatter that silence was the muffled echo of gloved hands being thumped together, and almost-rhythmic stamping of nearly-numb feet.

The sole topic of conversation, if anybody did feel inclined to speak to anybody, at that time of the morning, was to speculate as to 'what it would be today'.

The queue was soon strung out the entire length of the street, but as yet nobody had a clue what they were queuing for!

Whatever they guessed they were sure to have a twenty per cent chance of being correct. For it would be sure to be either one of the five basic foods. It would either be bread, butter, cheese, meat or sugar. It would certainly be one, and it would certainly be only one, of those commodities.

At five-thirty, however, and even at six-thirty, nobody knew which.

There was a bustle of anticipation as the door was unlocked noisily from the inside, at precisely seven o'clock. Soon the hitherto secret foodstuff of the day would be revealed!

The first customers to enter the shop surged forward to the counter, hands buried deep in their shopping bags. They had to find out what ration book to bring out. And as the first-to-be-served were being served the next to be served informed the hundreds waiting to be served in a kind of

Chinese whisper what it was they were actually queuing for.

That day it was butter.

Just before eight-thirty, and just after the bleak grey of the morning had dispensed with the raw black of the night, Joanna entered me shop. At least it would be good to be inside for five or ten minutes.

That shop had always intrigued Joanna, for the bizarre thing about it was that in addition to the product of the day, which was often also the product of the week, its entire stock consisted of only one grocery item.

Vinegar.

There were rough shelves spanning the full length of two of its walls and they were lined from end to end with one litre bottles of clear vinegar, two deep, and all covered in a greasy, dusty scum! The square-shouldered bottles with the fat, squat necks always reminded the imaginative Joanna of an army of some sort. Rank upon rank of identical shell-shocked soldiers, going nowhere, fighting nobody. Their days' work was to guard the long-suffering shoppers as they shuffled past their sentry post. Time and time again.

At least when you were in the shop you could always count the bottles to pass the time. And this Joanna did. Often. The total was always the same, though, every time she came. None of her neighbours ever seemed to actually buy any vinegar, and who could blame them. Who would want to sprinkle vinegar on their butter, their cheese, or even their bread?!

When she eventually reached the counter, the shopkeeper sliced Joanna off her ration of butter from a large irregular block of the stuff. When he had placed her portion on a piece of greaseproof paper he weighed it. One hundred and twenty five grams of butter was all that Joanna was allowed. One hundred and twenty five grams of butter was all that anybody was allowed, at any one time.

Having paid for her precious purchase, the young shopper stowed it safely in the bottom of her much too big bag, thanked the shopkeeper, and walked out of the shop. But not to trot off home for the rest of the day.

The snaking queue outside the shop by now stretched away out of sight in the sharp morning. Some of the neighbourhood's older residents, for whom five o'clock in the morning had just been too early, had begun to join.

Joanna walked along the whole length of the line, stopping occasionally to speak to someone she knew, for almost everybody had returned to speaking mode in the cold clear light of day. And when, at last, she reached the end of the queue, she simply joined it again! It would take her perhaps three hours to reach the counter once more, but when she did she could buy another one hundred and twenty five grams of butter.

It was butter today and perhaps there would be no more butter for three months. So everybody bought as much as they could possibly afford while stocks lasted. And when the stock ran out they all trekked home again until the shopkeeper took delivery of something else!

In mid-morning Thomas came across to take her place, allowing Joanna to go home for a break and something to eat.

Thomas and Joanna Maciantowicz were sensible, responsible children. They felt they had to be. Their parents had been divorced about three years previously, and they now lived with their father Michael, and his partner, Elizabeth, who had told them just to call her 'Auntie', and their toddler brother, Michael junior.

Although Elizabeth was very kind to all of them, Joanna in particular found the adjustment to this new style of family set-up difficult to cope with, and as a result, she and thirteen-year old Thomas had developed an almost adult sense of responsibility for themselves. And in an odd sort of an emotionally mixed-up manner, for the other three as well.

Joanna went back to relieve Thomas at noon, and stayed in that line, passing in and out of Vinegar Vigil, for the remainder of the day. Or at least for the remainder of the butter.

It was just after five o'clock in the evening when the shopkeeper locked up the shop, and the still-waiting worn-out would-be customers walked wearily away.

Joanna hadn't far to go to reach home. Less than five minutes took her back across the field and up to the third floor flat.

It was Saturday, and the eleven-year old girl had spent the greater part of her day off from school, standing in a line, just to buy butter.

It had all been worthwhile, though, for when she emptied out her big bag onto the little table in their little kitchen, she had five hundred grams, just over a pound, of butter. She had actually made it to the counter four times!

Next week, or maybe even next month, she might have the chance to queue up again.

And then she might be able to buy the bread to spread it on.

2

CROSSING THE LINE

Despite the hardships being endured by many in their country, Michael Maciantowicz determined that his family would have their usual and much needed family holiday in August 1981, if at all possible. And since they planned to be away for most of the month there had been a lot of preparation, which helped to fuel the anticipation.

Elizabeth had bottled meat and fruit in large preserving jars and Michael, father of the three children who were all so excited in their own way, and for their own reasons, assumed responsibility for procuring and testing the tents and an inflatable boat. Having long been a lover of the outdoor life it was a camping holiday Michael had arranged for them. In Poland's tranquil lakeland, in the north-east of the country.

It all sounded super!

On the day of departure everyone was up from early morning. There was so much to do! And look forward to! 'Auntie' Elizabeth carried out her carefully labelled boxes of food, Thomas and Joanna carried out, swung between them, bulging bags of clothes and sports equipment, and father packed the growing pile beside the car and trailer into the car and trailer. Little Michael junior just ran frantically up and down the stairs, carrying a yellow sand bucket and brandishing its matching spade, shouting gleefully, and tripping everyone, including himself, up.

The day was hot, the journey was long, and the car was crammed, but despite it all, everybody tried to be positive, thinking ahead, two hundred, then one hundred, then fifty, then only five miles to their destination, which would surely be idyllic.

When they eventually arrived there in early evening, they were not disappointed, either. It all seemed as picturesque and peaceful as it was promised to be. However, with the whole team busily engaged unpacking the car and trailer there wasn't much time to explore their new location that evening. By the time they had cooked something to eat, erected their tents, and spread out their groundsheets, it was time to flop down, exhausted, on to them. For it was dark!

It was not long after the sun had begun to brighten the interior of their tent next morning, though, that Thomas and Joanna were up and out to investigate what the campsite had to offer. For this campsite was set to be their home, hopefully, for the next four weeks.

What a beautiful place it was, too!

Their tent had been pitched just twenty metres from the edge of a large lake. The gentle rhythm of 'lake water lapping, with low sounds on the shore', had lulled Joanna to sleep on that very first night, and would do for many more nights to come.

A boarded walkway, which doubled as a slipway for the inflatable boat, stretched off out into the deeper water. When Joanna ambled out on that slatted decking in the stillness of the early morning she was amazed at how clear the water was. Every stone, every fish, every queer looking creeping thing, all legs and feelers, could be clearly seen for ever so far.

Except for their clearing, on which there were four tents, and a little sandy beach, about a hundred metres along from them, all the other shores of the lake seemed to be surrounded by dark-green deep-green blue-green pine trees, standing stiffly like sentinels, and stretching right down to the water's edge. Joanna was later to discover that on calm windless days, which was most days, the trees were reflected in the still water, and it was often difficult to distinguish from a distance where the shore ended and the water began. The whisper of the breeze in those trees, when the breeze chose to blow, had almost the same soothing sensation as the lapping of the water on the shore.

Up in a comer of their clearing was the forester's house and it, like the slipway, had a dual function, for it doubled as the 'camp shop'. With the forester doubling as the shopkeeper. All the campers were able to buy their fresh produce, especially eggs, milk and vegetables, from that enterprising individual.

As they settled into the site, everybody really began to enjoy themselves and relax. They found themselves able to shed in the sunshine, like a snake sheds its skin, all the haunting memories of the hardships, the shortages, and the queues of a difficult winter. In a place like this things like that were part of a long-gone and best forgotten past.

Thomas and Joanna were strong swimmers and they swam a lot in the lake. Three or four times a day was usual.

It was not forestry regulations, however, but uncle regulations, that imposed an artificial limitation on their water frolics. Their Aunt Mary and Uncle George were staying in another tent and Uncle was a keen and competent swimmer himself. He was also, though, very conscious of water safety, and the depths, and dangers, of their particular lake.

On his second or third day there, Uncle George took it upon himself to establish a sensible as he saw it code of conduct for their water sport activities. And as part of this he defined the outer limit for all family swimmers.

Inviting Thomas and Joanna to swim out with him that day, and as they trod water in a leisurely fashion, with the sunlight shimmering off the surface of the lake and on to their faces, he announced, "This is as far as any of us can go out in this lake. This is our boundary line."

He then pointed to a larger than usual pine tree at the edge of their clearing and went on, "Our limit will be the line between that big pine tree over there," and turning both his head and his pointing arm, continued, "and that rickety fence over there, coming down to the edge of the water from behind the forester's house."

Then, as they glided easily back toward the shore, Uncle outlined the proposed penalty for exceeding the understood limit.

"If I see either of you out beyond that line I have shown you," he told them gently but firmly, in adult it's all for your own good fashion, "you will not be allowed into the water again for three days."

Then after a pause, he added with a wry smile, "That is, of course, if you are not already drowned by then."

The ruling sounded fair enough, but it struck a defiant chord in Joanna's heart.

Even out here, she thought, in this wonderful, restful, place, there were limits. Boundaries. Frontiers.

Was there nowhere anywhere on this planet, where you could just go, or do, as you pleased? All the time? And for as long as you liked?

Michael Maciantowicz was a games coach, and if Uncle George was the self-appointed water sports supervisor, he had assumed the role of chief controller of land-based activity.

Just at the edge of the clearing there were two pine trees, all leaves at the top and all trunk at the bottom, standing some five metres apart, and it was between these trees that father hung a badminton net. And when they were not in the water swimming, by the tent eating, on the water boating, or in the tent sleeping, everybody was on the rough-grass half-dust makeshift badminton court, playing.

This was no let's just hammer the life out of the shuttlecock for the sheer fun of it, anytime we feel like it, kind of relaxation, though. To Michael, a fitness fanatic father, sport was serious stuff. And this badminton for his family and friends was no exception.

Partners were picked. Leagues were arranged. 'Court' times were allocated. Prizes were presented.

It was all meant for good fun, and Joanna, who loved games, mostly enjoyed it.

But if it was all good fun, it was not all complete freedom.

All the games were governed by imposed restraints.

Barriers. Boundaries. Again.

As the days progressed into weeks and the weather continued to be bright and sunny, day after day, Joanna, began to wonder why they had troubled to bring almost all the clothes they possessed, for she, for one, seemed to spend most of her waking hours in her swimsuit. She splashed in and out of the water, played badminton, and ran around all day in it. The only stage of any day when she wore anything else was late in the evening when the sun sank behind the pines casting a long straight golden glow across the lake. It was usually only then, in the after sunset sharp chill shock that she pulled on a T-shirt and a pair of shorts.

One day, towards the end of the third week in their camping paradise, everyone except Joanna left the site to go into the nearest town to search for essential supplies, not available in 'Forester's Supermarket'. Someone had to stay with the tents and all the gear and, for the first time, Joanna was trusted with that responsibility. She was over twelve now, and since the forester or his family were always around, it was considered safe to leave her.

Joanna was thrilled to be left in charge. It made her feel big. Mature. Important.

It was great for the first half-hour but after that she found that there wasn't much left for a twelve year old girl to do, on her own.

As she sat on the boardwalk, splashing her feet idly in the water, and relishing the warmth of the sun on her well-browned back, Joanna gazed out across the shimmering expanse of the lake.

It looked so inviting.

She stood up and walked slowly down the decking. And out into the water. When in to just above knee depth she propelled herself forward and with an easy, effortless, flowing movement, began to swim.

Out and out she swam. Farther and farther from the shore. The water was cold. And refreshing.

The sun was warm. And caressing.

All was calm. All was bright.

On and on she swam, until she reached the imaginary stop sign, the don't-cross line in the mind between the tallest pine and the broken-down fence.

Joanna ignored it completely and swam on. And on. And on. Out and away and beyond the boundary.

The water was just as cold, the sun was just as warm, and she was just as strong, as they had all been by the shore. So what was the difference? Why should she NOT swim on?

No reason, she concluded. And continued.

When she had almost reached the middle of the lake, Joanna stopped, and looked back towards the campsite. Then she began to swim lazily in a circle.

As she looked around, at the far away every way pine-lined shore she felt good somehow. Fulfilled, somehow. Grown-up, somehow.

A rising rebellious spirit in her felt satisfied.

She had crossed the line of petty restriction.

She had breached the boundary of imposed limitation.

Although her relatives had been doing their best for her, in a very difficult situation, Joanna had, in her just twelve years, felt in a certain sense let down, mixed up, messed about, and pushed around, by them, already.

Swimming along, alone in that lake, young Joanna Maciantowicz determined that what she had done that day was only the beginning.

She would continue to push beyond their borders.

She would break free. And be free. They would see.

Meantime, the most pressing thing she had to do was return to the shore. Before everybody else returned to the camp.

3

THE BLUE VASE

It was late December, 1981, and one of those dull, dark, cold and cheerless days between Christmas and the New Year. Martial law, with its rigid restrictions on distances travelled and group gatherings, its compulsory curfew times and prolonged school closures, had by then been imposed upon an already beleaguered country. So sunny days by shining lakes had become, for the Maciantowicz family, fond memories of a far-gone past.

Since their father and Elizabeth were both out at work, with some or other of them having left little brother Michael junior off at nursery on their way, and they were both on an enforced extended holiday from school, Thomas and Joanna had been left at home alone.

Although they had been left on their own, they had not, however, through the prior preparation of their attentive and well-organized father, been left to their own devices.

Every day, before he left, very early, for his work, Michael made sure that his older son and only daughter had something to engage their active minds or employ their useful hands, or both, in the hours stretching out ahead. A task to complete or a goal to achieve. And it would either be something practical to do, something educational to pursue, or something creative to inspire.

On some of the more mundane days the activity would be born of bold necessity, and dad's sense of order. The note of instruction would simply state, 'Today Joanna will hoover the house and Thomas will clean down the bathroom'. Essential, but not exactly exciting, employment.

The educational exercises were usually of a practical rather than a pore over books all day nature. One day it was, 'I have left you out a ruler. I want you to work out for me the area (length x breadth) of each room in the house, to the nearest square metre'. Joanna was glad of their father's original bent in the setting of their tasks. She didn't like pages of mathematics much.

By far the most appealing of all to the two inventive and imaginative Maciantowicz children, though, was when their father's to-do-today activity involved either writing a story or painting a picture. They had been asked, on a previous day, to write 'a description of a day by the lake in our holidays'. Joanna had been tempted then to write 'a description of a day IN the lake in our holidays', but she declined. The determination and resolution of that day were still very much in her mind, nonetheless. They had never gone away.

Another story which Joanna had really enjoyed writing, was the one about the dog. They had been required to write a story about 'A Poor Stray Dog' with the specific instruction, 'Make sure you find him a home'!

That had been fun!

What Joanna and Thomas tended to like best about those creative challenges was that they came in the form of a competition. With a prize. Both children were inclined to think that their dad had found some apparently genuine formula for fixing his results. For the prizes appeared to be awarded time about!

On the particularly dismal December day in question, the assignment which the long gone to work Michael had left for his two eldest children was an artistic, rather than a literary one. It was to draw and paint, rather than to compose and write.

When they were sufficiently aroused, awake and around to consider beginning their daily task, Thomas and Joanna consulted the note on the kitchen table, which said, 'You will find a vase of flowers on the writing-desk. I want you to draw and paint this as you see it. Today's prize will be an orange'.

In a comer of the boy's bedroom there was a large writing desk, the lid of which pulled down to give a work-surface of almost table size.

It was on the pulled-down leaf of this desk that the pair of aspiring artists found the vase of flowers.

There was a simple beauty about their father's foray into floral art.

A blue vase about twenty centimetres tall, with large looped handles like incongruous giant ears, stood in the middle of a square of starched white linen cloth, in the middle of the drop-down lid. The fattest, most bulged-out part of the vase boasted a single splotch of shiny gold. And the warm light from a single bulb glinted off the shiny gold, depending on your angle of view.

Carefully arranged in, rather than carelessly jammed into, the blue vase, were six or seven stems of wild purple heather. This collection of flowers represented at least one happy reminder of summer days or autumn walks, for they had been gathered on a trip to the hills at some stage earlier in the year, brought home and left to dry. Although by now almost crinkly dry the tiny bells of heather had lost none of their original strong purple colour. They still looked as though they belonged on the mountainside.

So that was their task. To draw, then paint, purple heather in a blue vase with big decorative blue handles and a distinctive gold spot.

In a relaxed, leisurely fashion they began. First they had to fetch their paint boxes from their schoolbags. Then jam jars of water from the kitchen. When they had satisfied themselves that they had all they required, work began. Again at a leisurely pace. They still had many on-their-own hours before them, and they weren't going anywhere, or doing anything, else. So they may as well take their time.

Although performed at laid-back pace, the work progressed steadily. The initial outline sketching, then the painting.

As they became more absorbed with the job in hand, there were less excursions to the bathroom or the kitchen, for nothing more than a change of position, and more diligent attention to detail.

In late afternoon, when the gloom of the winter day had been overtaken by the gloom of the winter night, the two paintings were complete. They sat side by side on the table to dry. And to await the verdict of the homecoming judge.

As Thomas busied himself emptying and washing their waterpots and brushes, Joanna stood staring at their 'works of art'.

She reckoned she had done well, and she had certainly tried her hardest, but her painting paled into insignificance when placed next to big brother's masterpiece. It looked wan and washed out beside his.

Joanna stood transfixed. The painting which Thomas had produced just looked to her like a Rembrandt or an early Picasso from the best gallery in the world. Every individual flower was so detailed, and the colours had been mixed so accurately and stood out so boldly, that the admiring little sister could almost convince herself that they were real. She wouldn't have been at all surprised if a big bee should suddenly bumble along and bump into them!

The shape of the vase, too, was so exact. So precise. Like a scale model. The fascinating thing about the portrayal of the vase was the manner in which Thomas had captured the glint of reflected light in the perfectly represented patch of gold.

It was wonderful!

When Thomas returned to the room, Joanna didn't say anything. She just gazed at him, almost through him, in worshipful envy.

'Oh boy, isn't he talented!' she thought. 'How I wish I could paint like that!'

When their father arrived home, just after six o'clock the two paintings were still lying, having completed their drying, where they had been left by the two all-day artists.

Before Michael even took off his overcoat he walked over and inspected his children's work. For two very sound reasons he had decided that judging should take place immediately. The first was to avoid any further suspense, and the other an eminently more practical one. He had the prize in his pocket!

Today there could be no question of a fix. And notions of rotation could not even be entertained. The winner of the competition was screaming up at him, "Bend down and smell my flowers! Can't you hear the hum of summer?!"

Thomas won the orange.

4

THE BIRTHDAY CAKE

Schools in Poland usually have a two-week winter break, and in 1982, for the schools around Krakow, this holiday was the last two weeks in January. For many families this winter vacation meant that children were merely forced to spend a further two weeks of cold, dark days at home, indoors.

Michael Maciantowicz, sports enthusiast, however, always planned, if possible, to have something different, something more stimulating, or more active, for his children to do in their holiday periods, whether summer or winter.

In January, 1982, it was, as it had been on a number of previous years, skiing. Michael had rented rooms in a huge log cabin up in the mountains, and left Elizabeth and the three children there to ski, every day. He drove them there on Saturday 16th, the first day of their holiday, stayed with them over the weekend, and returned to work Krakow on Monday morning. Before leaving that morning, though, he had promised, with a twinkle in his eye, that he would see them again, 'on Friday night'.

The mischievous glint in his eye was for a special reason, somebody felt. Father had it all worked out. So too, had that somebody else.

The next Friday would be January 22nd. And January 22nd was Joanna's birthday!

All week they skied. Elizabeth, Thomas, Joanna and even little Michael junior, set out every morning with their skis slung over their shoulders, their ski-boots and small lunches in their backpacks, to catch the bus to the slopes. Although Michael junior was still very young he was expected to ski along with the rest on the cute miniature skis his dad had bought for him on a business trip to western Europe.

It was exhilarating out in the cold crisp mountain air, day after day. Monday. Tuesday. Wednesday. Thursday.

Although Elizabeth and the other two children knew that Michael, their dad, had promised to return on Friday night they thought nothing more about it. He always returned on the Friday night of the middle weekend. Had never ever done anything else. He loved the speed and freedom of the ski-run, the clear sky above and the biting wind in his face, just as much as any of them.

For Joanna, though, it was different.

Riding on the bus, hurtling down the slope, or lying in her bunk during those warm and cosy minutes before she succumbed to sleep, her mind turned time and time again to Friday evening ahead.

On Monday, just after her dad had left she thought about it a lot. On Tuesday and Wednesday her anticipation still lingered on and off, but not so strongly. Thursday again became a day of unexpressed to the others, but real to herself, expectation.

What would Friday night bring? Would her dad remember her birthday? And if he did, what could he do about it? How could he buy her anything special in these days of rationing and scarcities?

It took her longer than usual to drop off to sleep that night.

Tomorrow would be Friday. They would ski all day and then father would arrive in the evening with … Well what? If … possibly … maybe …

But Friday didn't work out exactly as Joanna had visualized. Something over which none of them had the slightest control, occurred, to completely change the pattern for the day.

Elizabeth was first to rise that morning, and she came into the room in which the two older children had their bunks, with the news, "I doubt we won't be going up to the slopes today. In fact I doubt if we will be going anywhere today!"

"Why?!" Joanna was first to respond. "Why not? Why will we not be going anywhere?"

The hint of a smile flickered around the edges of 'Auntie's' lips. "Look outside," she replied softly, not directly answering the impetuous Joanna's spontaneous question.

Jumping up from her bunk Joanna rushed across to the window, wiped the condensation from it with a sideways slash of the side of her hand, and looked out.

And then she knew what Elizabeth meant.

It had snowed during the night.

And it was still snowing.

Huge flakes, like giant fluffy ping-pong balls, dropped slowly, silently, steadily, from a leaden sky, to land softly on the endless white carpet that was earth.

Joanna stood there, staring out, with a fixed, almost hypnotized gaze, at the mute majesty of the falling snow, for almost fifteen minutes. Until she began to realize that she was freezing cold! Then she dressed, with no sense of urgency.

Elizabeth had been right. They certainly wouldn't be going anywhere today!

As the day wore on and the children's fascination with watching ceaseless snow began to wane they turned their attention to other things. Like drawing, and playing table games.

Joanna's mind also turned to something else. Something personal. Her secret concern. What if the snow became so bad that the roads would become blocked? And travel would become impossible?

Such private anxieties were not at all helped either by Elizabeth's, almost hourly it seemed, predictions, that 'if that snow gets any worse your dad certainly won't make it tonight.'

Things changed in the afternoon. Took a turn for the worse, as far as the ill at ease, but trying not to show it, Joanna, was concerned.

A wind arose. It was the kind of thing you expected to happen in midwinter, but on that particular day it meant that the giant snowflakes which had been falling to earth in regular, direct, straight lines, began to approach their landing strip at an angle.

They blew along, almost unsure it seemed, of where to stop, like a light plane on a bumpy landing.

Looking out of the window in mid-afternoon, in the last of whatever daylight there ever had been Joanna noticed that snowdrifts had begun to form in the clearing outside their cabin. That's it finished now, she thought.

Father will never make it tonight. There is just no way.

When darkness had fallen they were all convinced of it. Michael wouldn't, Michael couldn't, make it …

At seven o'clock there was a loud knock, more like a thump than a knock, at the door.

"That will be the landlady," Elizabeth began, with a sigh, rising from her seat. "Probably a 'phone call from Michael."

The sound of the bang on the door had awakened within Joanna all the expectations of the week, and regardless of the fact that even she had accepted that they were by now ill-founded, she dashed to the door and arrived at it first.

She pulled the door open, helped in some measure by the swirling wind.

And there, outside, in the blinding snow, stood a snowman. But this snowman could blink, hold out his hands, and even talk!

It was Michael. Her dad!

His whole head and face were covered in snow. It even clung to his moustache and beard. The only sign of life on this literally snowwhite face was the blinking of its watering eyes.

The snowman held out his two hands. He had brought a box with him. It looked as though he had just nipped down from the North Pole to present the girl at the door with something.

"Happy birthday, Joanna!" the snowman said.

Joanna reached out and took the box from her dad, and by that time all four on the inside were out at the door.

There was great delight!

Joanna was so ecstatic that she didn't know whether to laugh or cry. She could hardly give her dad time to get his snow-covered great coat off for hugging him.

"Are you not going to open your box, Joanna?" he enquired. "Yes I am, when you are ready," Joanna replied, anxious that having come all that way on such a night, her dad should at least see her open what he had brought.

When she had set the box on the table and all the other four had gathered round, eyes agog, Joanna opened her box.

And in it was a birthday cake!

It was just no ordinary plain cake either.

It was beautifully decorated. The message of the day, 'Happy Birthday, Joanna' had been written across the white icing, in red. And over to one side of the greeting there was a single red rose, with two attendant green leaves. All made from icing!

Elizabeth, Thomas and Michael junior all just stared in amazement. Joanna cried, "Oh thank you dad! Thank you!" and resumed the hugging!

"Now we can have a party!" Thomas exclaimed, playing one last, long, loud chord on his guitar.

"Yes, that's just what we are going to do!" his father replied, his face red and shining, having come in to the heat from the snowy cold. "But before we do that there is something else we need."

Then, stepping over to his coat, which he had thrown casually over a convenient chair, he produced a paper package from his pocket.

What now? What next? The already awe-struck audience wondered.

From that paper packet Michael Maciantowicz, magic father, produced one at a time, one, two, three, four, five … right up to **thirteen** tiny candles in an assortment of pale pastel colours.

When he had them all out in his hand he passed them across to his delighted daughter with the suggestion, "These are for you, too, Joanna. Perhaps you would like to put them on the cake."

When she had done as her dad had asked, and had placed all the candles carefully on the cake, Joanna was almost in tears.

This was all so unbelievable!

The party began then and lasted well into the evening. It was such a pleasant time. Everyone seemed so happy. So relaxed. It was an opportunity to forget the storm outside and concentrate on one another. And Joanna. The birthday girl, seemed particularly at ease.

As she lay in her bunk, much later, though, she couldn't sleep. The performance of two people dominated her swirling thoughts. The first of these was her father. She just couldn't understand, and probably never would, how he had been able to do it! To procure a birthday cake, have it iced, and then as if by magic produce thirteen candles for it, in a country where they had to stand in line for basic foodstuffs, was completely incredible!

And as to how he had ever arrived at the log cabin in the mountains in such a snowstorm. Well, that was nothing short of a miracle!

The other person in her thoughts was herself. Joanna was compelled to recognise inwardly that she had inherited something of his spirit. She thought back to the sunny-day swim in the lake and recalled discovering that day what her dad had just demonstrated. That it is possible to go beyond the boundaries. And to weather every storm.

Everyone was trying ever so hard to be ever so kind to her. Why then did she feel so discontented? She still felt that she wanted to do her own thing. Be her own person. Stamp out her own identity, like footprints in the snow.

And after all, today was her birthday. She was thirteen now.

She was growing into a big strong girl.

She was a teenager now.

And teenagers sometimes have big strong ideas.

5

THE POND, AND BEYOND

Joanna and her two brothers loved the weekends, especially in spring and autumn. It was great to contemplate, through the long dragging days in school, that Saturday would be a family day away.

There were a number of interesting forest sites all within an hour's drive from home, and their dad would often take them all there on a suitable Saturday. In the morning they packed up enough food for the day, a ball or two, a few racquets, a net of some sort, and off they went. On arriving at their chosen spot, which was usually different every week, the three children collected some wood, their father lit a fire, and that forest clearing became 'home' for the next eight or ten hours.

On one such away-day in mid-September 1982, Michael senior, Elizabeth, Thomas, Joanna, and Michael junior were spending their day in the forest as usual. By late afternoon, having had a long walk in the morning, and an energetic game of volleyball after lunch, everyone was pleasantly tired, and left to his or her own devices an hour or so. Stretching out, idly kicking or batting a ball about, collecting firewood, wild flowers or mushrooms, or just wandering at will, were favourite pastimes in such periods. This respite would probably be only temporary, though, for doubtless their dad would have some all in together game or activity for them before packing up and heading home time.

Hopeful that there would be some spare time at some stage during the day to 'do her own thing', Joanna had half-heartedly brought her box of pastels and a sheet of drawing paper with her. She didn't know whether or not she would ever see a suitable subject to draw during her trip. It would be good to be prepared, though, in case she did.

The problem was that she had an art homework to do. And it had to be presented at the art class on the following Wednesday. The assignment had been to 'sketch the scene from the window of your home, or any other real life landscape'. It had to be a place where the pupils had been, and had actually seen, and most definitely not a copy of some faded picture on some faded wall.

The prospect of sketching 'the scene from her window' had not appealed to the creative thirteen-year old at all. To produce a picture of row upon row of Communist flats would not, she concluded, prove a particularly inspiring exercise. And anyway, how could she sketch blocks and block of flats that would be any different from anybody else's sketch of blocks and block of flats. For that was the view from almost everybody's window.

No, that was not for her.

Joanna, with her independent, imaginative nature, was determined to do, or at least try, something different. And out here in the forest she might even stumble upon a 'real life landscape'. One never knew!

While the other four were engrossed in their own interests, Joanna turned her attention to hers. Thomas had taken himself off into the silent depths of the forest to search for more wood for the fire. Michael junior had appointed himself chief poker and stoker of the fire, and had begun to prod at it with a long stick succeeding only in showering his father and Elizabeth, who were endeavouring to have a quiet chat, with showers of stinging sparks.

Leaving them all to it Joanna embarked upon her quest for a 'real life landscape' for her homework, with a folding chair in one hand and her paper and pastels in the other.

What will I ever find to draw she wondered?

Having gone not more than one hundred and fifty yards from the focal fire, Joanna spotted a small pond. This was not any big lake. Nor was it even a small lake. It was more like an overgrown, outsized, quite deep puddle.

There was something about this tiny stretch of water that instantly arrested the on the look out would-be-artist. It halted her in her tracks.

Attracted her entire attention.

Joanna stopped, set up her chair, and sat down.

As her eyes swept across the scene before her, she seemed to stop breathing for a moment. It was as though she was temporarily transposed into a state of suspended animation. Life, and the world, stood still for a split second.

The whole vista was so awe-inspiring, and just screaming to be sketched. It was pleading to her paper and her pastels!

A number of elements, common to many a forest scene, had in that moment, and at the spot where Joanna had stumbled upon them inadvertently, woven themselves into a tapestry of simple, but striking, beauty.

On the horizon were rows and rows of dark green pine trees dissected by a curving forest track which disappeared into a single distant point amongst them. That was the background, the outer framework, for the scene.

The really exquisite beauty was closer at hand, however. And it lay on the surface of the pond.

Being an incredibly still, sunny, autumn day the surface of that pond was like a mirror. White fluffy clouds scudded across a bright blue sky, and the reflection of those white fluffy clouds scudding across that bright blue sky, presented a perfect mirror image on the top of the water. The airy lightness of those scampering clouds, each one of a totally different size and shape, hurrying across the lake on their obviously urgent business, fascinated Joanna. And the fact that the contrast in colour between the blue of the sky and the white of the clouds was stronger in reflection than in reality, held her spellbound.

There were other shapes, and colours, in that simple show, staged by nature, too.

Many years before, a tree had fallen in at the corner of the pool, and the heat of successive summers followed by the frost of successive winters had seen it stripped of all its leaves and bark. It was now nothing more than a pathetic skeleton, a shadow of its former self, with bleached white branches which pointed stark accusing fingers at the sky above and the forest beyond. Every one of these blanched branches was perfectly mirrored in the plate-glass water, as well.

Then there was the rich red of the ripening holly berries tucked into the deep green shelter of their fiercely prickly protecting leaves, on a solitary bent-over bush five yards from the pond on its farther bank.

Only the tip of this bush had made it on to the mirror.

Tiny yellow flowers, woody bunches of purple heather and three flood-water-rounded stones were scattered at random around the marshy margins of the mini lake.

These all helped provide tiny specks and flecks of contrasting colour in the picture on the pond.

It was all just magic. And Joanna was magnetised by it.

After having soaked up the scene for ten minutes, marvelling at its overall impact, Joanna began to sketch it carefully with her pastels.

This, to her, was infinitely more alluring than the drab and dismal scene from her window.

For an uninterrupted hour, Joanna worked on that sketch. She became completely absorbed in it. Every shape, every colour and the whole general atmosphere of tranquil beauty cried out to be recorded in minutest detail.

When she had finished her homework Joanna was pleased. And her pleasure stemmed, too, from more than the mere sense of relief at having another homework ticked off in her diary. There was a deep sense of satisfaction. And ultimate achievement. The young artist felt that she had somehow captured forever, on paper and with pastels, something wonderful which would never ever appear exactly the same again.

Her dad was awaiting her return to the 'home' base, his curiosity understandably aroused by her unusual protracted absence. Although he knew where she had been he was interested to find out what had kept her wrapped up for so long.

"And what have you been doing with yourself this last hour and more, Joanna?" he enquired, with a smile.

"I was doing a sketch. For my homework," his teenage daughter replied, trying to sound as matter of fact as possible, when she was, and probably for the first time, secretly proud of her artistic effort.

"Are you not going to let us see it then?" Michael persuaded, always interested in his children's activities.

Rather shyly Joanna produced her labour of love and her dad seemed instantly excited by it. "Come here everybody and see Joanna's drawing!" he called out spontaneously to the others who were tidying up to go home in unhurried, easy-going fashion.

When Elizabeth and her two brothers bustled across to see her work they all seemed impressed with it also.

Michael junior, summed up the reaction of them all with typical childish candour when he exclaimed, "Hey Joanna, that's great!"

The big test was still to come, though. On the next Wednesday afternoon. In the art class.

When the pupils were instructed to put their homework out on the table before them, Joanna produced her 'pond and beyond' sketch.

The teacher, who had been walking up one row and down the next, inspecting everyone's work, passing comment here and there, stopped stock still beside Joanna's desk.

And there she stood motionless for all of half a minute, as though paralyzed.

Other children in the class turned around to see what had happened to her.

Then, after quizzing her pupil as to the location of her compelling 'real life landscape' she went on to remark, "You know Joanna you ought to seriously consider applying for Art College."

That was, without doubt, the highest tribute that could be paid to a thirteen-year-old schoolgirl. That her art teacher considered her honest endeavours to be of Art Academy standard!

Later that evening Joanna told Thomas of her teacher's comment and he was thrilled. "Tell you what I will do, Joanna," he enthused. "Two of my friends are very artistic. Indeed one of them, Derek actually goes to Art College. When you have done a few more drawings then I will invite him round to have a look at your work. And we will see what he thinks!"

Three weeks later, when the by now enthusiastic Joanna was satisfied that she had a reasonable variety of art work produced Thomas kept his promise. And asked his friends to pay them a call, at home.

This, for Joanna was a very big occasion. A student from Art College actually coming to give his 'expert' opinion on her very amateur art! She could hardly have been any more excited had the President of Russia or America or some of those big and powerful faraway places phoned to say that he was calling to pay her a state visit!

When Derek and his friend, who were both still teenage artists themselves, came around and viewed the mini-exhibition of first paintings which Joanna had draped all around the living-room, they were, as had been her family, and her teacher, by her 'pond in the forest' sketch, instantly inspired.

"Joanna, you should definitely go to Art College!" the student of that prestigious school exclaimed unreservedly when he had carefully studied all that she had to show him. "That work is wonderful!"

Then, later on that year, three different things happened, involving three different members of the family.

Joanna, through her school, submitted an application for admission to Art College.

Her dad, just to satisfy himself about this talent that people had started to talk about, arranged to take his daughter to visit the studio of a well-known artist whom he knew, one Saturday. This artist, Anthony, having watched Joanna paint for part of the day, went into the room where her dad was patiently awaiting his verdict.

"Well what do you think Anthony?" he enquired. "Should Joanna go to Art College?"

"It's not a case of should, Michael," his friend replied, emphatically. "Joanna MUST go to Art College!"

And Thomas, whose blue vase painting had so affected his younger sister, moving her almost to the point of tears about a year before, began his High School career. Majoring in mathematics!

6

ONE MORE NUN LESS

The first five months of 1983 were a period of frantic activity for the by-now-fourteen-year-old aspiring art student. She had to submit a folder of art work, in a variety of mediums, before the end of May. Joanna was not alone in this, however, for almost five hundred other eager and talented young people had been asked to do exactly the same thing!

Krakow Art College was renowned for the high standard of the education it provided and hence obtaining admission to it often proved difficult. Competition for the fifty places on offer each year was extremely keen.

When she had submitted her folder Joanna thought that she would hear no more. That was it. What hope had she amongst so many?

All the applicants had been informed that from the five hundred folders submitted the College staff would select one hundred students to sit the four-day entrance examination. Then, based on the examination results a final selection would be made. From the one hundred entrants, fifty would be chosen to enrol in the College.

With such stiff competition Joanna had tried not to build up her hopes. She kept thinking of her teacher who had recommended that she should apply for a place. Then it dawned on her that all the other applicants were probably so gifted that all their teachers had probably recommended that they should apply for places too!

What chance had she?

In early June, then, she was half-surprised and wholly delighted to receive a letter inviting her to present herself, at the College, on a certain specified date, to sit the entrance examination.

That was thrilling! She had made it into the last twenty per cent of the applicants. But could she make the last fifty per cent of the last twenty per cent?

That was now the question.

On the first day of the examination Joanna found herself seated beside a fourteen year-old lad. His name, he said, was Jacob.

In the edgy excitement of that first all-dressed up and with pens pencils and paints all at the ready morning, they began to talk.

Although they would both sit the complete cross section of subjects in this entrance examination, Joanna had applied to follow the course in painting, whereas Jacob hoped to specialise in sculpture.

As they talked, though, neither of them was too confident of anything. They discussed their proposed courses. Why they had chosen them. And why they would probably never see them!

"These examinations are supposed to be very hard," Jacob reported. "One of my friends didn't pass last year. He said they were awful. And he is really smart, too!"

"Yes, I know they are," Joanna replied. "I have heard that also. There is no way that I am going to pass them!"

"I won't pass them either," her fellow-fatalist responded with a resigned sigh, adding, "But I suppose we have done well to make it this far!"

"If you don't get into the Art College what will you do?" Joanna went on to probe. She had her own idea about that. For herself. It would be interesting to hear if Jacob had a Plan B. An emergency exit, if he didn't make it through. And he was sitting beside her at that moment declaring most definitely that he wouldn't!

Jacob gave a peculiar, nervous, not very sincere-sounding laugh.

"You will never believe it," he went on, as though honestly expecting her never to believe it, "but if I don't get into this College I think I will join the ZOMO."

Joanna looked across at him quizzically.

"The ZOMO?" she repeated. She was having difficulty believing it. Why would a friendly lad like this want to join the despised and dreaded special police whose job it was to suppress any opposition to Communism?

"Yes," Jacob reiterated, with a mischievous twinkle in his eye, "The ZOMO." Then, not wishing to be asked any further questions, he went on to turn the tables on his slim and tall for her age soft spoken companion, who was still busily trying to determine whether or not he was joking.

"And what about you?" he enquired. "If you don't pass what are you going to do with yourself?"

She had a feeling that this question was bound to come sometime, and since Joanna had thought the matter through often in the will I won't I? previous six or seven months, she had her answer ready.

"If I don't go to Art College," Joanna told him, "I am going to be a nun."

Although the statement tripped off her tongue lightly, almost flippantly, Joanna was only half-joking.

It was now Jacob's tum to be surprised. He was astonished almost.

"Surely you wouldn't want to do that!" was his immediate and instinctive reaction. "Shut yourself off from everybody for ever and spend all your time saying prayers and things!"

Although he could not have realised it, Jacob had touched right upon one of the reasons why this girl would want to become a nun. She had often imagined it would be a relief to shut herself 'off from everybody for ever,' as Jacob had expressed it. That, she fancied, would be a marvellous way to opt out from all the pressures of life. From all the disappointment and disillusionment. And from the endless simmering below the surface dissatisfaction. Some of it caused by circumstances without, but most of it stemming from conflict within.

For not only was Joanna beset with tensions in the strained relationships of her day-to-day living, but she was also torn apart with a personal sense of inadequacy, inferiority, and lack of self esteem.

Although she was just about to sit an entrance examination for one of the most prestigious Colleges in Krakow, Joanna had never been completely satisfied with herself somehow. There had always been that sense that something was missing. It was as though there was a great gaping hole down deep inside her, and no matter how many pleasant thoughts or experiences she tried to shovel into it, that hole never even began to fill up. It was always there. Gaping open. Swallowing her up, from the inside out.

It was a spiritual vacuum which Joanna, despite her every frantic effort, always failed to fill.

Perhaps, she reasoned, if she became a nun the incessant involvement with church and creed would plug the hole. Stop the gap. And help her find, for the first time in her life, satisfaction with herself, and peace in her soul.

Indeed, if she was not accepted for the College, she just might become a nun.

Joanna and Jacob had many more conversations during the next few days, as they sat an assortment of examinations, designed not only to determine the applicants' abilities in different artistic disciplines, but also requiring the demonstration of a high degree of competence in the core subjects of Polish and Mathematics.

After their four-day side by side stint of painting and printing, composing and calculating, the two had become quite friendly.

As they parted on the final afternoon Jacob quipped, "Goodbye Joanna. It was great to meet you. But I think after those examinations I will never meet you again!"

Joanna felt much the same about him.

Next week though, they would know.

On the day on which the results were to be posted up in the huge hallway of the Krakow Art College, Joanna's dad went out, alone, to ascertain his daughter's fate. He considered it potentially too painful for her to go along with him, or worse still to go along herself, just in case of disappointment. Although he had always tried to convince himself that his Joanna was very talented, there would be ninety-nine other sets of parents up at that educational institution who would no doubt have come to similar conclusions about their sons or daughters long ago, as well.

When he entered the College vestibule Michael had no trouble finding the notice-board with the results posted up on it. A crowd of anxious parents, some of them accompanied by their anxious offspring, milled before it.

As they discovered whether they had passed or failed, whether they were being admitted or rejected, whether they were 'in' or 'out', the crowd of either delighted or devastated teenagers with their either delighted or devastated parents, gradually dispersed.

Eventually Michael made it to within reading distance of the notice.

There were two lists. One for painting. The other for sculpture.

Knowing that Joanna had applied for the painting course her dad naturally focused his attention on the 'painting' list. And he automatically looked down at the middle of the list. He was searching for M for Maciantowicz.

He looked. And looked. And looked.

There were other M's down about the middle where they should have been.

But there was no Maciantowicz.

There was no point in standing there any longer. Much as he would have loved to take a pen and write his definitely gifted daughter's name on that list, he couldn't. There was nothing he could do.

Anyway his eyes had become so blurred with tears he was incapable of seeing the list any more.

Joanna's dad peeled off from the side of the crowd, and lit a cigarette. He would have to give this matter some careful thought.

Whatever was he going to do?

And whatever was he going to tell Joanna, who would, by now, be expecting him home? She had worked so hard for this, and had produced such a wonderful portfolio of paintings.

This news would break her heart!

There was a row of chairs along one side of the entrance hall. The deeply disappointed father sat down on one of them to consider his next move. As he sat there, contemplating twenty or thirty gentle ways of saying the same sad thing, Michael looked around.

This was such an impressive place. It just dripped character. Wouldn't it have been wonderful if Joanna could only have been a part of it?! What a sickening shame!

When the ear-piercing clamour of excited voices and the muted solemnity of muffled sobs had all passed out through the broad front door, Joanna's dad was left alone. In awesome silence.

He would have to go. Joanna would have to be told. Somehow.

Just before he left, however, he decided to visit the notice-board one last time. Perhaps he had missed something first time around …

And he had.

There it was!

MACIANTOWICZ, Joanna.

Her name was at the very top of the list. The examination results had been posted in merit order, not alphabetical order, as he had expected. And his Joanna's name was at the top! She had scored the highest marks of all the applicants for the painting class, and so she had been the very first to be assured of her place in the Art College!

Michael ran out of the hallway. And soon he was home to tell his worried daughter the wonderful news!

The devastated turned delighted dad had missed one thing, though. Not that he cared. Not that it mattered to him. But Jacob was side by side with Joanna again. His name was just across from hers. At the top of the list for the sculpture class!

They had both been accepted. The pair who had encouraged each other, and commiserated with each other, all through the week of the entrance examination had both passed. At the top of their respective classes!

So there would be one more ZOMO less in Poland!

And one more nun less too!

7

PRAYER AND POPPIES
ON THE PILGRIMAGE

In September Joanna commenced her studies in Art College. This, for her, was the fulfillment of a dream, for it was then that she began doing what she most enjoyed doing. This was painting. The only down side to her studies was that she was expected to squander precious painting time on insignificant to her subjects like Polish, Mathematics and English as well.

During that first College year the new all fresh and keen student became very involved with life in the Roman Catholic Church. She and her friend Eva began to do jobs for others, helping them through church work-schemes. For although Joanna loved her painting she was even willing to devote some of her precious spare non-painting time to helping others in the hope that such selfless dedication and kind deeds would somehow help dispel the void, block up the blank, deep in the heart of her.

It was a fruitless dream.

It didn't.

While she was engaged in all sorts of helpful activities which were very much appreciated by the elderly lady on whom Eva and she lavished such care and attention, Joanna began to read a little book of New Testament stories which someone had given her. One night, after reading that booklet, she was overcome by emotion and wrote in her diary the simple but heartfelt words, 'Jesus, I love you!' Perhaps this open expression of affection towards Jesus, whom she barely knew, but understood to be someone gentle and good, caring and compassionate, far away, yet someone to whom she felt strongly and strangely attracted, would help fill the growing-greater gap at the centre of her being.

It was a fruitless dream.

It didn't, either.

Then in June of the following year, just as Joanna was about to complete her first year at college, she and Eva discussed something which they had heard announced in Church. There was to be a summer pilgrimage from Krakow to Czestochowa, a city some one hundred miles to the north, and a kind of spiritual mecca for the Roman Catholic church in Poland. Everybody and anybody who wanted 'to enhance their spiritual lives' was invited to join.

The two girls greeted this as 'a great idea.' As they contemplated a pilgrimage they became ever more enthusiastic at the prospect.

Just think of it. They were going to get away together for a week, on a sort of holy sort of holiday, and it would allow Joanna to spend time out from the external pressures of home and the internal pressures of her own making.

Above all there was always the possibility that this project could provide the solution to her perpetual and perplexing problem.

Could Joanna find peace on a pilgrimage? Perhaps.

She would give it a try. And Eva was happy to go too.

The summer pilgrimage, when the much anticipated date for it came around, began in an air of muted, sacred excitement. Two hundred people, both young and old, from babes in arms to crocks with sticks, assembled in Krakow, all eager to set out. Each pilgrim carried a small back pack containing a little food, a change of clothes, and the essential bottle of water.

It had been made abundantly clear in preparation classes that on this pilgrimage the emphasis would be solely on the spiritual, and not at all on the physical, well-being of the participants.

Joanna and Eva were as excited as all the others at the beginning. When the motley group began singing and praying its way through the stopped-traffic streets of their home city and northwards out into the countryside, they felt strangely elated. Joanna, in her long flowing dress, printed all over with gaudy sunflowers, her multiple strings of all different lengths of brightly-coloured beads, her brilliant yellow bandanna streaming out beside or behind her, and her consuming passion for personal peace, felt proud to be part of it all.

That first day was fine. All prayer and praise and promise. And soothing summer sunshine.

Then that night they slept on stacks of straw in a farmer's barn. What a big adventure!

The second day and night were much the same. So much to see, and hear. So many sincere people to talk to. A few faltering older friends to encourage.

And ceaseless summer sunshine.

By the third day, however, the unrelenting heat and increasing exhaustion were beginning to tell on the two teenage pilgrims.

Joanna began to feel sick. Then she lost her appetite. Nasty waves of nausea rolled over her at the very thought of food. She felt tempted to pack it all in and take the next bus back home to Krakow. But didn't.

One of the organisers offered to take her along in the car for a mile or two. But she refused.

This, she thought, was where it was doing her so much good. All this self-imposed physical persecution was probably purging all the sin and impurity out of her.

So she struggled to continue, singing and walking, praying and walking, singing and walking, praying and walking, endlessly.

In the searing, sickening, summer sunshine.

It was on that third day, too, that Joanna and Eva were befriended by a young couple. Their garish hippie style dress and bright and breezy personalities must have identified them as possible partners, and this young pair invited them to share their tiny tent that night. Very kind of them, the two tired teenagers thought, so they accepted the invitation. It would be a relief to sleep on a groundsheet for a change.

What happened that night, and on succeeding nights, in that tent, came as a culture shock to the two young girls. A crude contrast to their perception of the purpose of the pilgrimage. They were soon to discover that this friendly couple, who were in their early twenties, and who sang and prayed so sincerely and passionately during the day, had a totally different agenda at night.

While everyone else was preparing to have something to eat, and then settle down for the evening, this young pair invariably set off for a walk.

They wanted to be away, on their own, 'for a period of private prayer and meditation'.

They wanted to be away on their own, it was true, but they were not seeking to conquer some spiritual summit. They were planning to have their 'highs' another way!

Joanna had been so glad to lie down after what had been the most gruelling day to date for her, and she and Eva were just drifting off into the refreshing realm of restful sleep when their new host and hostess arrived back from their deepening dusk into early dark excursion.

The two friends slowly returned to semi-wakefulness. They had to. The tent was small, and its owners didn't seem to have any immediate plans to even lie down, not to mention go to sleep. They kept taking more and more precious groundsheet space, forcing their teenage guests right out against the outer canvas.

It was then that Eva and Joanna found out why they had been away for so long. They hadn't been visiting a prayer sanctuary in a nearby village, but a poppy field they had noticed as they had passed along earlier with the pilgrims, and obviously considered worth a closer look.

They had pouches packed with the poppy seeds they had picked.

Then, later on, when the only sounds from outside were the occasional voice raised in a solemn chant, and the far away braying of a distant donkey, and they were as sure as they could be that they would not be disturbed, the real business of the night for them began.

By a crude and complicated method they began to extract opium from the seeds. When they had eventually procured enough of the liquid to satisfy their requirements, they then proceeded to inject each other with it, sharing a non too hygienic looking syringe. The two teenage spectators were surprised, even shocked, to realize that these two apparently deeply caring and apparently-profoundly religious people had come on the pilgrimage equipped for the poppy fields! They had all the gear with them. Syringes, a band to tighten around their arms, and various other pieces of paraphernalia, whose function Eva and Joanna never quite fathomed.

On their second night of tent-sharing the poppy seed pickers offered to extend their generosity by sharing not only their dwelling, but also their drugs, with their new friends.

Joanna and Eva refused. Immediately. And emphatically. Neither girl had any inclination towards participation. They knew that this surreptitious night-time activity was not right, and certainly not in keeping with the day-time spirit of the pilgrimage.

This complete contrast between the midday and midnight activities of this drug-shooting couple filled the impressionable Joanna with a disturbing sense of disillusionment. As she walked along on the succeeding days she found great difficulty in joining in with all the seemingly so sincere prayers and songs of praise.

Her mind had been hi-jacked by another matter.

She was wondering what all these other singing-praying-people were doing at night.

Did everybody here have double standards?

It was probably unfair of her to think that way, for most of them seemed genuinely engrossed in their worship.

But she could never seem to rid herself of the question that kept bumbling around in her brain. After the light-time, bright-time, day-time, did any, or many, of these people have a dark-time, black-time, night-time side to their lives and characters as well?

Joanna was deeply disappointed.

Terribly disillusioned.

So much so that she and Eva didn't return home for two days after everyone else had departed back to Krakow.

They decided to 'freak out'. The two teenage companions, now tired and bedraggled, stayed another couple of days in Czestochova. The pilgrimage had taught them how to survive living rough. So they made the best of that piece of practical information.

It was only when their food and money ran done, and the creative call of the paint-brush and palette became too strong for Joanna to resist, that the two unfulfilled pilgrims returned home.

On the journey southward in the train Joanna felt thoroughly depressed. Utterly dejected.

She had hoped that a week of pilgrimage would provide her with the personal peace she so constantly craved.

It hadn't.

8

THIS IS GENIUS!

When Joanna went back to College in September to commence another year she discovered that she had a new teacher in one of her painting classes.

During the awkward shadow-boxing first day of students sizing up their new teacher, and teacher attempting to size up yet another batch of new students, the latest member of the teaching staff did what many would have done in his position.

He made a request of them, and assigned them a task.

He wanted to see what they had done. And what they could do. His aim was two-fold. It was to assess ability. And explore potential.

When he had spent some time in early evaluation he would then be more adequately equipped to target his teaching at an appropriate level.

"What I want you to do for me for next week," he told his latest class, towards the end of that initial session, "is to bring me in a representative sample of your last year's work, say six or eight pieces. Also, I want you to do me a painting and a pencil-line drawing illustrating your memories of the summer."

There was a short sharp sigh from some of the students. Here we go again, they thought. Back to the old teacher's favourite. Some of them felt that they had been writing descriptions and painting pictures of all their summer holidays every September since they were seven.

For Joanna though, it was different.

She had some very vivid memories of the summer. And painting was her pathway to expression.

Walking home from school she allowed the images of the summer to flip over in her mind, slowly, and then slide on past, like the pages of a book slipping through her fingers, regarded then discarded, when searching for some precise piece of information.

The temptation always was, on such occasions, to portray the summer as she would have liked it to have been, rather than as it actually was.

Joanna had not long arrived home until she began to sketch. She struggled at first to depict in a drawing the summer as she had remembered it. For what she was trying to illustrate was not so much an image as an aspiration.

Page after page of early-planning paper was drawn over and set aside. Soon the piled up pages spilled over. Some slid off her desk and skimmed across the floor.

And still Joanna sketched.

Slowly but surely, in her churning yet creative mind a means of summarising her summer had begun to crystallise.

It amounted to a visual description of a desire. For it was the picture of a purpose.

It took days, and many abortive attempts, before the young art student was satisfied that she had faithfully represented, with one single pencil, on one single page, her condensed recollections of that summer.

But when it was complete she was content with it. For it accurately pictured her unceasing quest for ultimate peace.

At the foreground of the picture was a girl, dressed in a long flowing frock. The girl's face could not be seen. Just her back. And on that back was a tiny rucksack. The light wispy hair of the subject floated and drifted gently around her shoulders, creating the impression of a gentle summer breeze.

Stretching out ahead of this girl there was a road, down which she was obviously gazing. This was a long road, a dry road, and a dusty road, but a road that stretched right out across the page. From the girl's feet to the distant horizon.

And it was the depiction of that distant horizon that Joanna had spent so long to perfect. Time and time again she had tried it. And time and time again she hadn't been happy with it. But now she was. For now she felt she had pictured it properly.

Very skilfully Joanna had used the converging lines of a tree lined road to give the impression that the gazing girl was focusing on one particular point in the dim distance. That point was a beautiful shining castle. Shafts of light from it streamed and streaked across the far-off cloudless sky.

Her completed picture comprised only the three main elements. There was a pilgrim, a road, and a shining castle.

There was a seeker, a journey, and an ultimate, and eventually attainable but as yet-unattained goal.

That was Joanna's summer. In a nutshell.

As she pulled together her bits and pieces before leaving home on the morning of her second lesson with her new teacher, Joanna looked again at her pencil sketch. It stirred again within her a tumult of memories of those hot summer days on that pilgrimage. And although there had been at least two hundred others going through that experience with her, none of them featured in her picture. For she had no idea how they had felt then, nor could she ever hope to have any idea of how they felt now. But she knew how she felt. Still unfulfilled and far away. And her picture was of her summer.

She understood all that. What would her teacher think of it, though? Would he even understand what it was all about. Was it all a bit too mystical? Rather too obscure, perhaps?

The painting class began with the collection of everyone's homework.

Before going around the class to inspect the samples of his students' earlier efforts in art, which they had been told to leave out available on their tables, the teacher arranged all the new material in a display across the front of the classroom and part way down one side.

Then threading his way among the tables, he bent down to pick up a painting here and there, and commented on the colour or the contrast, the depth or the dimension of it, with its creator. When he had passed her table, having made some appreciative noises, Joanna felt free to survey all the work around the walls.

And it was then that she wondered if she hadn't missed the mark completely in her home assignment!

For all the pictures except hers seemed to be of clearly definable places, many of them containing clearly definable people doing clearly definable things. There were mountain lakes, crowded beaches, a busy fairground and quite a number of the Rynek Glowny, Krakow's large and lovely market square, of which the city's residents were so justly proud, with its Cloth Hall, old clock tower and numerous colourful pavement cafes.

Her simple but striking sketch of the lonely pilgrim on the lonely road to lasting happiness stood out in stark contrast to all the other presentable pictures of the perfectly obvious.

What on earth would the teacher make of it?

When the appraisal of each student's individual portfolio was complete the teacher re-established himself at the front of the room and the group evaluation of the newest additions to their classroom exhibition began.

One by one they were discussed. The teacher encouraged all the students to have their say on whatever aspect of a particular painting or drawing pleased them.

Depending on the subject of the picture, or the medium in which had been created, matters like foreground and background, perspective and texture, and in the case of the many drawings including a number of Krakow's magnificent buildings, line and style of architecture, were duly deliberated upon.

Then, after what seemed, to Joanna, an interminable time talking about trivia, her latest teacher stepped across in front of her latest drawing.

And there was silence. Absolute silence.

The teacher just stood there staring. And absolutely speechless. After what must have been a full minute the class began to become shifty. And shuffle about.

Why was the teacher not talking?

He wasn't talking because he had taken another step. But it was forward this time. He wanted to read the name scrawled in the bottom left-hand comer.

Eventually he turned, and looking Joanna straight in the eye, he asked, "And who is this figure in your drawing, Joanna?"

Recognising that all her classmates would have been aware of the annual summer church pilgrimages, the slightly-blushing student replied, "It's a pilgrim."

The teacher smiled. He had another question. "Is the pilgrim you?" he enquired, gently.

Joanna let her head drop a little. She could feel her face burning now.

"Yes. I think it is," she confessed.

Sensing her embarrassment the teacher reverted his attention to her drawing.

Then, after another significant silence he spoke again, his soft words laden with calculated sincerity.

"This is genius!" he muttered. "This is genius!"

9

DIARY OF A DYING GIRL

As she progressed through teenage Joanna derived increasing pleasure from her involvement in creative expression, including not only painting, her first love, but also sculpture, drawing, printing and photography.

The ability to produce individual creations, praised by her teachers, granted her a sense of fulfillment.

That, though, was her singular source of any delight.

With almost everything, and almost everybody, else, she felt totally disenchanted. She felt personally unfulfilled, inwardly absolutely empty.

What was the point of everything, or indeed anything, anyway?

After the pain of the pilgrimage with its attendant disappointment and disillusionment, Joanna vowed to herself that she was finished with church outings. She would be going on no more of them. Her previous disagreeable experience would be her only disagreeable experience. Definitely.

The following summer she found herself relenting, though. And the pattern was the same as it had been for the painful pilgrimage.

Eva and she had heard an announcement in church about an Oasis camp for teenagers, at a retreat centre, set high in the beautiful Tatra Mountains of southern Poland.

Thus despite Joanna's passionate never no more pledge of the previous year, the instant reaction of the firm friends had been, "Let's go to that!"

The very thought of it sparked off an irresistible daydream in the imaginative mind of an artist. Mountainsides dressed in forests of pine trees in different shapes, and shades of green. Deep pools in silent streams. Dashing, splashing, white-foamed waterfalls. Birds soaring, gliding, dipping and rising, on the gentle summer breeze. She could almost feel the crisp, clear air chilling its way down into her city lungs, as she contemplated it!

They would go.

And they did.

Nor were they disappointed in the location. It was just as Joanna had visualised it in her many expectant fantasies. Exactly. A clutch of cabins high in the mountains. Twenty teenagers from various places who had decided to attempt an escape from the rigours and pressures of the world below and seek at least temporary respite in that haven in the mountains.

The camp had not been organised to provide the young people with a week of carefree abandon in idyllic surroundings, however. It had been planned with a spiritual purpose in mind. To make everyone more aware of God. In his creation and goodness. It was to be a time of purposeful reflection and meditation.

In an attempt to aid towards this end, special days were designated. One was a day of fasting.

Joanna didn't find that too difficult.

She was not a big eater anyway.

Another was a day of walking, and talking. Of praying and praising. A single day of pilgrimage.

Joanna found that more difficult.

Her problem was that in spite of the fact that all the young people around her, with many of whom she and Eva had struck up really good friendships, seemed genuine, she kept remembering the drug shooting charlatans of a year before.

Another was a day of silence.

Joanna found that the most difficult of all!

For Joanna loved to talk! She enjoyed lively conversation and would talk animatedly to her new friends of four days about anything and everything except the utter unhappiness of the hole at her heart.

She viewed the prospect of a day of silence with a slight sense of apprehension.

What was she supposed to do all day when she couldn't communicate with her friends?

Think, was what they had been told was the purpose of the exercise. Think. And communicate with God.

Joanna had often thought about her thoughts. And thought that she thought too much about her thoughts. Her penchant for incessant introspective evaluation of every thought and feeling, every action and reaction, was part of her problem, she often concluded.

Now she was going to have a whole day of it! Wow!

The day didn't turn out as badly as Joanna had dreaded, however, for throughout the day one person was permitted to speak, but only at meal-times. And she was only permitted to read from a pre-arranged book. Something which had been deemed appropriate to the situation.

There were to be three reading sessions. The silent consumption of meagre breakfast, meagre lunch, and meagre evening meal, was to the lilting read accompaniment of a touching story.

The short book was the diary of a dying girl.

At breakfast time the diners had heard of the girl's initial reaction to the fact that she had been diagnosed as having leukaemia.

Lunch time had brought her personal coming to terms with the ups and downs of the disease. The trauma of the treatment. The hope of a cure.

It was at the evening meal, though, that the story which had already gripped the soul of the speechless Joanna, had the most profound effect upon her. For it was at that final session that the girl in the story gave her reaction to the news that there was no hope. That her cancer was incurable. That she was going to die.

'My family are very distressed,' came the voice of the fluent reader, echoing across the hushed and cramped dining quarters. 'They are all trying not to let me see them crying, but I know that they have been. They can't hide it. I just keep telling them not to worry about me, for when I die I will go immediately straight into the eternal arms of God.

'Don't be sad for me, I say. Be happy. For I will be happy. Don't weep for me for days when I die, I say. Be joyful. For I will be joyful. Safe in the strong arms of the eternal God.

'And then when you die we will all be together again. With God. Forever.'

It was Joanna's turn to help with the clearing up after the meal. And she had indicated, by a series of not-too-serious mimes, that she would wash the dishes.

Her mind had a lot more questions to cope with now, though, as she worked.

She had a lot more thinking to do.

As she sloshed the water around the plates which she kept piling into the froth-filled sink with her froth-framed hands, she wondered, 'How is it possible to be so confident in the face of death?

'How could anybody, but especially a twelve-year old girl, have such faith in the future?

'And that was another question she had never ever carefully considered before. The future. Is there a life after death? A beyond?'

It was the sense of serenity and security about the dying girl's declarations that had most impressed the dumb-for-the-day dish washer.

She had talked about being happy. About being joyful. And about 'the strong arms of the eternal God.'

As Joanna placed the last plate out on the drying rack for some mute dryer to pick up, she did so with an unusual defiant determination.

'Why had she that strength?' she wondered.

'How could she be so sure?

'There must be an answer.

'And I must find it!'

10

REFRESHING NIGHT!
INSPIRING DAY!

That summer of challenge at the Oasis camp was followed by an autumn of discontent.

As the evenings became shorter and colder, and the leaves on the trees encircling Krakow's city centre, turned red and golden and fell into either crispy and crinkly or slimy and slippery carpets on the ground, Joanna's mood began to reflect the season. She became colder towards others. And more gloomy in herself.

Although she was a popular student at college she preferred to walk home alone. Deep in thought.

And to spend hours alone at home. Deep in thought. Shut up in her room. Shut off from the others.

The lonely blackness of an impending winter had begun to infiltrate her soul.

Joanna would arrive home from college late in the afternoon and go straight to her bedroom. Repeated attempts by other members of the family to coax her out, or to persuade her to eat, all proved pointless.

Trying to talk to her was a futile exercise, too.

Joanna wasn't going to pour out her heart to anybody, partly because she didn't trust anybody any more, and partly because she wasn't quite sure exactly what it was that was wrong with her in the first place.

Her only solace was to pour out her heart in her art. Paint, a brush or crayons, paper or a canvas, were her confidantes. She allowed the secrets of her seeking soul to stream out through them.

One night in late October, Joanna decided that she would just paint, and paint, and paint. What was the point in going to bed? She probably wouldn't sleep anyway. Or if she did chance to fall asleep she would be plagued by the most horrendous nightmares.

She was desperately seeking spiritual satisfaction. But where was it to be found?

The production of pleasing paintings gave at least visual satisfaction. They offered an aesthetic, if not the constantly craved spiritual, gratification.

It was almost nine o'clock when Joanna lit her candle, and placed it beside her easel and began to prepare for her marathon paint-in.

The first subjects of the evening were the autumn leaves she had picked up idly and flattened into her ever-present folder on the way home that afternoon. She closed the lid down over the keys of the piano in her room, and placed the leaves on the lid. When she had arranged them to her pleasing she began to paint.

There was no hurry. By ten o'clock all sound in the flat had ceased. Everybody was in bed. Except her.

Eleven o'clock came. And went.

Just before midnight the first picture was complete.

Every leaf in that collection had been selected for some particular reason. And it showed in the end. As she stepped back from the easel to survey the finished work, the night-owl artist sensed a warm glow of pleasure flowing over her.

It looked well. It was very striking.

Leaves of different shapes, in a total range of autumn colours from fierce fiery reds to glowing golds, and in a total range of textures from the geometrically-patterned roughly-ribbed to the shiny perfectly smooth, seemed to want to leap up at their painter from the paper. Each leaf had gained an equal and opposite, too, for each leaf had its own painted reflection, as it appeared immaculately mirrored in the polished black lid of the polished black piano.

Joanna's enjoyment of that first of the-night painting spurred her on to further effort.

Her next project was different. There was something which she had always promised herself she would do, but had never yet done. And what better time to do it, than when she had plenty of time, in the middle of the night?

This painter loved poetry. And for years she had been planning a water-colour painting in muted colours of a book of poems lying open on a desk or table. That, to her, would symbolise the creative beauty of literature.

So why not do it now?

When she had cleared a space on her desk, she began flicking through one of her few precious poetry anthologies with the intention of selecting one of her favourite poems, at which she could leave it lying open during the painting process.

Then she became absorbed. She read snippets from one poem. Snatches from another. Whole poems in places.

Having long since appreciated that poets were merely painters with words, Joanna spent forty minutes allowing the clever collection of word and thought, in rhyme with rhythm, in sonnets and stanzas, to flood into and over her mind.

It was refreshing. And exhilarating.

And now she was about to paint a picture of her book …

For more than an hour she worked at that, sketching lightly, then painting in soft colours.

And again when she had finished, the result was instantly gratifying. She had successfully represented in one sketch the two loves of her life. Painting and poetry.

When she glanced over at her clock which nestled in the dim distance at the other side of the room in the flickering candlelight, Joanna realized that it was just past three o'clock in the morning.

Everything was so still and quiet. There was no sound of anything or from anybody. The world seemed ever so remote and removed. She was ruler of her own little isolated realm. And nobody else mattered.

It made her feel good.

Nor was she going to bed yet, either. There were still more than four hours to go until time to rise to go to college! She just might make it to bed. That time, if it came, would be later, though. There was so much still to do!

As night wore on towards morning, however, Joanna began to tire. The candle smoke and constant concentration were beginning to have an effect.

There was just one more drawing she wanted to do, regardless of how tired she felt, and that was a sketch of her college building. And for this she chose a different medium entirely. Charcoal.

Placing a large sheet of paper on her easel Joanna began to draw in bold black lines. Columns, windows, doors, paths, trees around. Then when she was sure that her drawing accurately represented her college building she added the final embellishment.

For some reason the in the black of the night artist surrounded the college building with birds. Big black birds, with big black beaks. They were walking on the college lawns, perched in the college trees, swooping through the above the college sky. Horrible, ominous, big black birds.

When she stepped back from that charcoal drawing Joanna felt somehow briefly fulfilled. She hadn't a clue why she had drawn what she had drawn, but she liked it. For it said something. Something deep.

As she placed her charcoal sticks back in their tin she wiped her fingers on a duster and then looked towards the window. Chinks of light were sneaking below the drawn-down blind. Dawn was breaking. It was almost six-thirty. And time to go to bed.

Leaving the big black birds in charge of her easel, Joanna slipped into bed for an hour. Then she was in a position to rise, when called.

While crossing the hallway to go to the bathroom later she met her dad, who greeted her with a cheery, "Had you a good night, Joanna?"

"Yes, I had a most refreshing night!" came the reply …

Most mornings on her way to college Joanna called at the house of a friend, also called Joanna. The two girls usually walked together to college, and sat together in classes.

It was one drab mid-November morning, just three weeks after the 'refreshing' paint all night experiment, that Joanna flopped down on a chair in her friend's house as Joanna the second went in search of her shoes and socks.

"I don't feel like going to school today," Joanna called through to her friend who was bustling about in the bedroom. "This is the day when we have a double period of that awful Army Training and a double period of Chemistry. I am fed up with all that stuff. All I want to do is paint."

"Well then, don't go to school today. My folks are away and won't be home until late. You can stay here if you like," came the called back, slightly breathless reply.

Joanna stood up.

"Do you mean that?" she continued.

"Yes, of course I mean it," the other Joanna replied, arriving back in the living room, all duly dressed for departure. "If all you want to do is paint, then just stay here and paint. You can use my paints and easel. I will see you when I come back in the afternoon. Easy."

That proposition required some consideration. Joanna had never skipped classes before but to stay there and paint was a lot more appealing than sitting through lessons in Army Training and Chemistry. And English. What on earth would she ever need to know English for?!

"Yes, Joanna, I think that's a brilliant idea," she concluded at length. "I will just stay here and paint. Then when you come home it will be time for me to go home!"

Five minutes later the outside door closed with a resounding clonk. One Joanna was outside, on her way to college. The other was inside, on her way to a day of nothing else but painting.

Like as in her night of painting, so in this day, there was no rush.

It was now just before nine o'clock in the morning, and she had at least until four o'clock in the afternoon to paint. What bliss!

At leisurely pace she set her friend's easel up in the middle of the living-room floor. Then she clipped on to it the biggest piece of paper she could find.

Joanna had an idea. And it was the full length mirror on the back of the door out into the hallway that gave her the idea.

'I will paint the biggest self-portrait I have ever done', she decided. Again she was attempting to look at herself. To come to terms with herself. Why was she so sick of herself? Why could she not be bothered with people, or even, as she had just discovered, with Polish, any more? Why did she just want to be left alone, with her problems and her paints?

When she had prepared a palette of paints she began her self-portrait. This was fun. Seeing herself as others saw her, but portraying herself as she wanted to be seen. There was a balance to be stuck in there somewhere.

Shortly after eleven o'clock the doorbell rang.

Joanna jumped!

She certainly hadn't been expecting visitors.

Was that Joanna's father back? What was she going to do? Perhaps it was just the postman. If she ignored it perhaps he would go away …

But whoever it was didn't go away, for the bell rang again, seeming to echo all over the flat.

Joanna knew she couldn't ignore that second call. Perhaps it was somebody about something important.

She went to the outside door, and edging it open gingerly, peered out into the corridor. And there she saw something that immediately struck her as funny.

Standing there was a girl of about fourteen years of age, but small for her age. She had the collar of her overcoat pulled up tightly around her and she was clutching it tightly below her chin.

It was what she was holding in the other hand, however, that had forced Joanna to see the funny side.

For with her right hand she was strenuously balancing a massive musical instrument case which was easily six inches taller than herself!

"Isn't this where Joanna lives?" she enquired shyly of the stranger who had come to the door.

"Yes," Joanna replied. "This is where Joanna lives. And I am Joanna, too."

The tiny teenager with the big box looked at her quizzically. "Well, the other Joanna said I could come to her flat and spend the day here," she went on … "I am from the Music College and I just want to practice. I am sick of the endless theory."

"Come on in! Join the club!" Joanna invited, laughing heartily. It had been her first real laugh for days, but she was both amused, and relieved. What if it had been someone from Art College looking for her? Or the other Joanna's dad? Or the police?!

As the new arrival struggled to steer her colossal case past Joanna's nearly life size self portrait, the artist and first truant pointed to the case and asked, "What have you got in that thing?"

The child with the case flopped down into the chair that Joanna had been sitting on earlier and replied with a puff, "It's my cello!"

Joanna returned to the easel and her self-portrait.

Then, when she had recovered both her breath and her composure, the guest musician opened her case, took out her cello and bow, set up some music, and began to play.

Within minutes the haunting strains of some pieces by Johann Sebastian Bach were floating through the flat.

Joanna was entranced. She had always loved Bach, and now to have his music played by this tiny, but obviously talented cellist, was an unbelievable bonus!

The day, from then on, passed so quickly.

When the artist felt like taking a break she set down her brush, and complimented the sweet music, occasionally requesting yet another piece.

When the musician felt like taking a break she set down her bow, and complimented the progressing self-portrait, making occasional helpful, but not always heeded, suggestions.

By the time Joanna the absentee hostess returned, shortly after four o'clock, the pair who had never met before in their lives, had become firm friends, the relationship cemented by a recognition by each of talent in the other, and a shared passion to immerse themselves in their own speciality.

Reluctantly Joanna rolled up her completed self-portrait and placed it in her folder. It would make an interesting addition to her portfolio at the end of term. She then thanked her namesake for her hospitality, said cheerio to the cellist, and walked the short distance home.

When she opened the front door, her dad, who had just arrived back before her, and was always interested in his daughter's wellbeing, but had been worried lately about her attitude and behaviour, called out from another room, "How was your day, Joanna?"

"Oh I have had an inspiring day!" his daughter replied.

Father was pleased.

That was a step in the right direction.

It was marvellous to hear Joanna sounding so positive again.

Little did he know where she had been!

Or why she felt so inspired!

11

NAME ABOVE ALL NAMES

Later on in that year a new girl joined the painting class. Joanna and she struck up an instant friendship and it didn't take her long to discover that this new girl with whom she had begun to share a double desk in most of their classes, had something curiously charming about her.

There was a magnetism about Majka.

Joanna hadn't spent many days in her company either until she had uncovered the secret of her singular appeal.

"Have you ever been to the Dominican Church, Joanna?" Majka asked the kind girl who had tried to make her feel welcome in her new environment.

"No, I haven't," Joanna confessed quite candidly. "My church is farther out from the city centre."

"Oh, you ought to come to us! Especially in the mornings!" Majka exclaimed, obviously animated. "We are seeing a marvellous movement of The Holy Spirit amongst us!"

That was a new one on Joanna. The Holy Spirit. It sounded just a little bit sinister to her. A *holy* spirit? That *moved*? How? Where? When?

Despite her difficulty with the definition, she refrained from expressing her ignorance. Instead she just continued to listen.

For Majka had much more to say.

"Every morning, before I come here, I go to the Dominican Church," she explained. "There I meet with a lot of other young people. We go there every school morning at seven o'clock to Mass, to pray and sing praises to God. I suppose it is some people's way of protesting against Communism. As for me, I just like to worship. Everybody probably goes for their own good reason."

That was interesting.

And Majka was ever so sincere about it all.

Perhaps that was how she could fill the increasing emptiness of her life. She should become all fired up about something, like this fired-up friend. Come out against Communism. Show somebody where she stood. Do something drastic or different.

Thus when the enthusiastic early morning church attender invited Joanna to 'join me some morning just to see what it's like', she was ready to respond. If these dawn of the day meetings gave Majka such pleasure, left her so excited, perhaps they would do the same for her.

She went the next Monday morning.

New week. New experience.

And for the seriously mixed-up soul of the certainly talented teenage artist that spring morning held a few surprises.

The first gentle jolt for Joanna was the attendance. Majka had arranged to meet her and accompany her on that introductory morning, and as they approached the Dominican Church they were joined by many other young people, both older and younger than themselves, all hurrying along. They jarred the early-morning hush with their happy early-morning hubbub. Some of these were children, pushing up into their early teens. Others were obviously university types. Most of them carried with them, with differing degrees of ease and comfort, at least one of the trappings of learning. Bags, or untidy piles of books and files, instrument cases, sports gear, and art folders were all in evidence.

It seemed to Joanna as she and Majka mingled in with the others, that most of the educational institutions in Krakow seemed to be represented. There were far more people than she had ever expected out in the early morning, and on their way to church.

Why? She wondered.

What was so special about this? Was it merely an effort to stand up and be counted against Communism, or was there more to it than that?

When they entered the church building it was the atmosphere that immediately arrested the latest arrival. There was something warm and welcoming about it. Joanna felt immediately at home. A man in his early twenties was playing a guitar and leading the arriving, settling congregation in singing. Everyone seemed to be joining in. Some were raising their hands. They all looked so comfortable. As though they were there because they genuinely *wanted* to be there, not because they had been forced to be there.

The third surprise for Joanna, on that trial morning, after the attendance, and the atmosphere, was what lay, still undiscovered by the new recruit, in the tiny mass room at the side of the church.

Majka had something else for her new friend to see, and to enjoy, before they set off for their day at the desk and the easel.

"Come on down into this little room over here," she invited, pointing to a door from which two lads and a girl all about their own age, had just emerged. "We will have something to eat before we go."

"What do you mean?" Joanna was puzzled. And looked it. "I have already had something to eat before I left the house!"

"That was a long time ago now! Especially for a big girl like you!" Majka joked, looking up at her much taller friend. "Come on!" and with that she led the way.

When she had duly followed her in, Joanna found that the centrepiece of the small adjoining room was a long table. This table, which took up most of the available space in the room, had been covered with a white linen cloth.

On the cloth had been place bread and milk. A lot of it. Three-quarters of the table was covered by large trays of fresh crispy morning rolls, which had undoubtedly once been stacked neatly, but now after having been under constant attack, lay in healthily haphazard heaps. They had just been freshly baked. The smell of them was wonderful.

The remaining quarter of the table was home to a number of jugs of milk in varying stages of fullness or emptiness, depending on how you looked at it. And beside the jugs a very much great number of glasses. Many of these had already been used and had been left aside to be washed. There were four stacks of clean on left.

Bouncing across to the table Majka repeated her invitation.

"Come on, Joanna, help yourself!" she called out cheerily. Then as though to demonstrate how it was done she did exactly that. She helped herself. To bread and milk.

The meal was modest, but mouth watering. Pleasingly plain.

And Joanna helped herself, too. As she had been invited to do!

That was the start of it!

She and Majka began to meet every morning and go to the seven o'clock praise and prayer and then bread and milk service in th Dominican Church together.

It was there, too, about two weeks later that Joanna heard the words of a chorus that she couldn't get out of her mind …

As the leader announced the chorus and then began to play the chords on his guitar Joanna felt that there was something special about this particular tune. It appeared to have an exceptional appeal to her as an individual for it immediately permeated every cranny of her tortured mind in some strangely soothing way.

Then came the words. Simple words. In short lines. But they struck Joanna with such force that she found herself compelled to analyse every one of them. Over and over again …

'Jesus, Name above all names,
Beautiful Saviour, glorious Lord,
Emmanuel, God is with us,
Blessed Redeemer, Living Word.'

As the crowd of young people began to sing, Joanna was captivated. The melodic combination of the words and tune had a profound effect upon her. It must have had the same effect on the leader, too, for he called out, "That was lovely! Let's sing it again!"

They did, and when they had finished he called out, "Again!". So they sang it again.

Joanna felt like shouting out, "Just sing it for ever. Don't stop!"

For the remainder of that day, and for weeks afterwards, that chorus and its tune were always close to the surface of her consciousness.

Whether on a bus, in a class, on the street, or in bed just drifting off into sleep, she found herself thinking about those words. And asking herself endless questions.

Why was Jesus, 'Name above all names?' What made Him so special? He certainly seemed to be very important to Majka and some of the early-morning crowd at the Dominican Church.

Then she thought of 'Emmanuel, God is with us'. Was God with her? No.

Baby Joanna with her mother

Krakow Main Square, Joanna's home town

Colin, age 11

Northern Ireland, Colin's country

...The Childhood Years!

Colin and his six brothers

Joanna with her mother, father and brother Thomas

Joanna with father, step mother Elizabeth and brothers Thomas and Micheal

Joanna with uncle George and aunt Mary, and brother Thomas

Joanna with her brothers on Polish holidays at Baltic Sea

Colin's Mum with the twins Colin and Edwin

Drawing one of the first sketches during family picnic

Colin's family with their 2 cousins

Skiing in Poland with Joanna's father

Colin, age almost 17

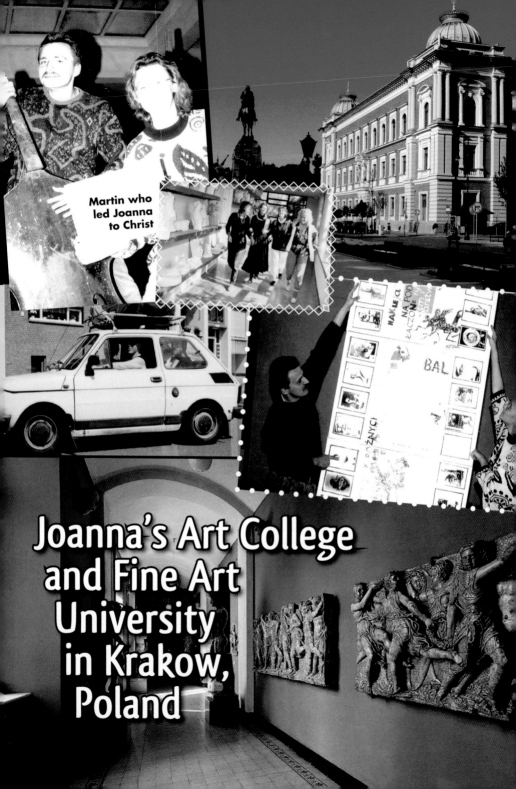

Martin who led Joanna to Christ

Joanna's Art College and Fine Art University in Krakow, Poland

Old town of Krakow, near to Joanna's university

9th of May 1994, Joanna received Masters Degree in Art

Joanna's home town

Exhibition of Joanna's diploma work in Poland

Krakow Main Square by night where Colin and Joanna met

Colin in Venice, just weeks after meeting in Poland

Just days before Joanna met Colin

The time we met...

The window where Colin and Joanna met. Photo taken in August 2013.

Poppy field in Poland

Colin, Ian and Gary
on the Berlin wall,
2 days before
meeting Joanna

Polish mountains during
the weekend Colin and
Joanna met

Polish horses at work

POLSKA

KOCHAM CIĘ

TO
COLIN TINSLEY
1 BALLYMACWARD RD
DUNDROD, CRUMLIN
CO. ANTRIM
BT 29 4JB   N. IRELAND
(PÓŁNOCNA IRLANDIA)

**Colin's letter to Joanna
written on 21.03.1994**

---

21 MARCH 1994

Dear Joanna
 At this present moment in time,
I'm sitting in my car down a county
road near my house. Its 12.00 midnight
The first day of British Summer is
just over, its a beautiful night with
a full moon so quiet and peaceful the
lovely light, frost just covering the ground
 Today is Sunday I'm just back
from church a couple of hours ago. I
go to church every Sunday morning and
night. I enjoy it very much. I became
a Christian when I was 17 years old.
By doing this I simply excepted Jesus
into my life by prayerfully saying
Into my Heart - Into my Heart - come into
my heart lord Jesus, come into day
come in to stay come into my heart
lord Jesus. By doing this my sins
were washed away and my night was
turned to day since Jesus came into
my heart. I now own him as my lord
and Saviour. Hes my best friend. I give
him all my problems and pray to him
often. It a nice felling, a personal love

**Joanna's letter to Colin
written on 7.04.1994**

X You tell me in your last letter
that you became Christian when you were
17 years old. That's great that praying to Jesus
gives you so much. The time we spend
with Jesus is so important. He is the one
to whom we can believe to, and we
can follow to. He is the only and the
best to follow his example.
I had a long way to find him,
though I'm Christian since I was born
and baptized in the age of 1 year.
You can't be Christian by name
You must be Christian by the heart.
My story is pretty long, I'd like to tell
you when I see you. It is so very much
important to me. For few years, I totally
lost the way to Jesus. I couldn't find
him. I felt very bad with that,
sometimes I didn't think of it, sometimes
I almost cryied. I started to feel a
very painful wound in my heart.
Then, somewhere on the horizon I saw
the light. I started to move toward
it, though I still had so many doubts
I was meeting some friends, talking
to them about it. I asked them
to pray for me, because I still doubted
and still could not understand how
good is Jesus, our lord. It took a long
long time, and suddenly one day
came. One of my friends came to visit
me and we prayed together at my
home. I felt exactly what I must to
do. I felt I must invite Jesus to my
heart. I felt I need him like nothing
else. And that was it! I'll tell you
some more about it. I hope it will be
very soon. I already would like to be
X in Ireland.

To/
By air mail
Par avion
le Shuttle
FOLKESTONE

SOANNA MACIANTOWICZ

UL. NAD. SUDOŁEM
24/7
31-228. KRAKÓW

POLAND

3

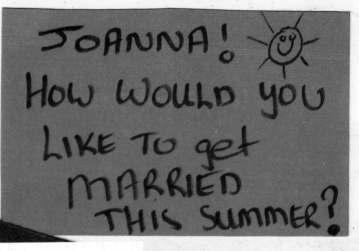

JOANNA!
HOW WOULD YOU
LIKE TO get
MARRIED
THIS SUMMER?

COLIN,
DARLING,
I LOVE YOU
SO VERY MUCH
AND
I CAN'T SAY
ANY OTHER
WORD THAN...   ... YES

The heart shaped potatoe that Colin posted to Joanna from N. Ireland (chapter 33)

CUSTOMS/DOUANE CI

COLIN TINSLEY
1 BALLYMACWARD R.
DUNDROD CRUMLI.
Co. ANTRIM
N. IRELAND
BT29 4JB

(May be opened) (Peut être ouvert
officially) d'office)
Detach this part if the packet is accompanied by a
Customs declaration. Otherwise it must be
completed.
See instructions on the back.

Detailed Description of Contents
(Désignation détaillée du contenu)

1 potatoe

Value (Valeur)   Net Weight
(Specify the currency)   (Poids net)

COLIN TINSLEY
BALLYMACWARD RD.
DUNDROD, CRUMLIN
Co. ANTRIM
N. IRELAND
BT29 4JB

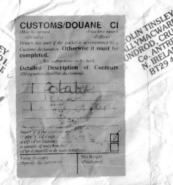

Cactus blossom (chapter 31)

Colin's dad giving Joanna away

The Tinsley family

Mum and Dad

Wedding in N. Ireland

Continuing in Poland

Prayer in Baptist Church in Krakow

One of the places visited during honeymoon

Rainbow above our mobile home

First years together

First house

Donegal

Working on the 'Tangled Lamb' with the author Noel Davidson and his wife Liz in Poland 2000

One of the tangled lambs

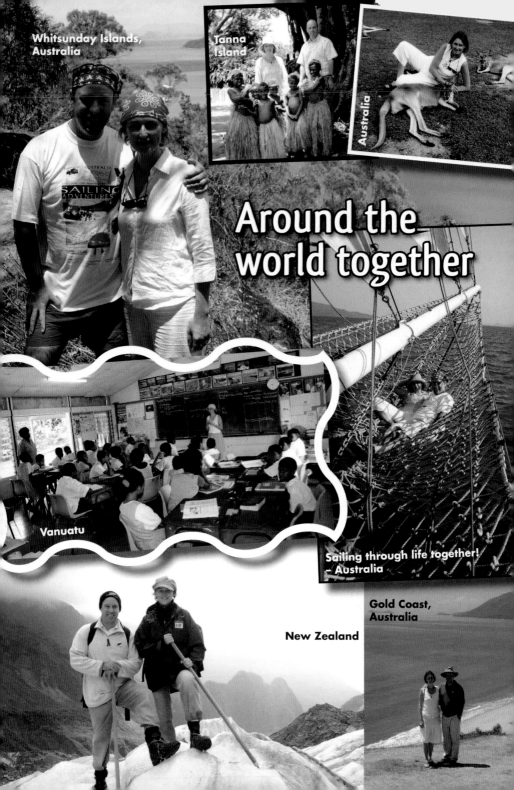

Whitsunday Islands, Australia

Tanna Island

Australia

Around the world together

Vanuatu

Sailing through life together! – Australia

New Zealand

Gold Coast, Australia

The Tinsley family

Joanna and her mum

Joanna's parents visiting N.Ireland

She is forever mine!

In our house with Mum and Dad

THIS HOLY BIBLE IS

PRESENTED TO

Joanna Kocham cie Ptaszku????

BY

Colin xx "He loved her" Gen?

ON

10th September 2013

twenty years after we met in

Kracow on that beautiful eve

10th Scptember 1993

She didn't think so. For if He was, surely she wouldn't feel as sick at heart and as totally inwardly unhappy as she did.

And Blessed Redeemer. What did that mean?

Or Living Word? Who, or what, was that?

As she contemplated this beautiful chorus that she sang and hummed at all kinds of odd moments, Joanna decided that there was a spiritual message, which as yet she did not understand, in it for her.

I don't have a faith. A goal. A purpose in life, she concluded one day.

But she yearned for a living faith, and a positive outlook on life.

One night, before going to sleep, she sang the chorus softly to herself, and then prayed, softly, "God, if You are really there, and this what I have been singing is really true, please show me how I can know Jesus, Name above all names, and have You with me. Please let the Living Word, whoever or whatever it is, speak to me."

As she lay back in bed, and closed her eyes Joanna had the sensation of being at the end of a long, dark tunnel. Somewhere, ever so far away, at the absolute far end of the tunnel, there was a penetrating pinprick of light.

Somehow she felt that she had touched eternal truth.

But there was so much she still didn't know.

The tunnel was very long. And desperately dark.

Someday, somewhere I will reach that light, she vowed.

How, though, or where, or when, were all also things which she still didn't know.

Yet.

12

THE DEATH MACHINE

Just when she imagined that a glimmer of light had begun to glow at the end of her tunnel of darkness, just when she imagined that possibly 'Jesus, Name above all names' could somehow provide a key that would unlock the door into everlasting light, Joanna was plunged, for a few days, into unbelievable blackness again …

It had been a tiring day at college and she had been painting until late at night. Having no desire to repeat her previous all night session, she slipped into bed shortly after eleven o'clock, and was soon in a sound sleep.

Although her body was at rest, however, her mind wasn't. It was racing.

That night Joanna had the most bizarre dream she had ever experienced. It was most fantastic, but frighteningly realistic.

She was the only person in the dream. The sole actress in a most alarming drama.

In her dream Joanna saw herself, dressed in one of her favourite long white dresses. She was not bedecked with any of her usual way-out accessories, though. There was no gaily-coloured bandanna wafting in the wind, and there were no almost tripping her strings of beads, in glass, or wood, or amber. None of that. She was just wearing a long, plain, white dress, that seemed to shimmer softly in a strange light.

Dressed in that simple attire, she visualised herself walking slowly, but steadily forward. There was a sense in which she felt herself more than walking, but actually being involuntarily impelled, forward, by some invisible but irresistible influence. It was like what she had read about in pirate stories, 'walking the plank'. Being forced forward at the point of a sword, with neither the ability or the facility to turn around.

As she progressed in her mandatory march she could see up ahead of her the top of a most complicated machine. There were pulley wheels of various sizes and big black belts coming up from some low-down location which she couldn't yet see. These belts were driving the wheels around at terrifying speed.

Suddenly, and simultaneously, Joanna the dreamer, became aware of two things. One was the sweet scent around. The other was the five steps down.

While she had been moving ever onward, the scene around her had gradually changed. Now the woman in white was trekking through a most beautiful sunlit wildflower meadow. Flowers of every hue, from the stark red and black of the poppies, to the bright yellow of sunflowers in all sizes, from the unusually small to the six-foot tall, and purple heather, all jostled for position. All the flowers were from some part of her past and they all bent towards her, bowing gracefully as though acknowledging that, as she passed along, unstopping, on her compulsive path.

The aroma all around was marvellous, too. Sweet fragrance filled the air. It smelt like an almost overpowering blend of freshly-crushed lavender and heavily scented old-fashioned cabbage roses.

Yet still she was driven inexorably ahead. Towards the five steps down.

On approaching these steps Joanna discovered that they led down towards the base of the vast complicated machine, most of which she could now see. There were now dozens of belts, and wheels, and chutes and shafts. Bursts of steam spurted forth from different parts and in no set pattern.

The noise was deafening. A loud, monotonous endless clanking.

And Joanna had started to go down the steps. Towards it.

Soon the field of flowers and the refreshing fragrance were all left far behind.

Now she was descending. Towards the mouth of the machine.

Stepping down from the third step, Joanna noticed that a cavernous hole had opened at ground level. Strange ever so white smoke to match her ever so white dress, formed a constantly changing arch at the entrance to this weird contraption.

And still she went forward. Powerfully propelled.

On, and on, and on …

Through the smoke-encircled archway, and into the cavernous depths of the machine she marched, in almost military fashion.

All light had faded now.

Blackness, a blackness that she could almost feel, enveloped her.

The clanging and the clanking, the hooting and the hissing had all stopped too. There was no noise now at all.

Nothing.

Just total and absolute eerie silence.

Slowly she felt herself becoming stiffer and colder. And falling backwards.

Now she wasn't walking any more. She didn't need to. She didn't have to …

In a few more seconds the dreaming Joanna emerged from the other end of the machine. Her face had now lost its colour. It merged with the ever so white of her dress.

All life had left her body.

What that stone still clinging white-clad corpse came out into wasn't light. Nor was it dark. It was a state of boring boundless grey, stretching away, away, away …

Through this nondescript nothingness the lifeless body levitated. Gravity had gone. The corpse began to float farther and farther towards infinity.

What was going to happen now? …

Joanna woke up with a start.

She was trembling and holding on to a crumpled lump of sheet with frantic hands.

Her first reaction was to heave a huge sigh of relief. At least she was still alive. She hadn't passed through the death machine which her dream had so dramatically depicted.

For weeks, though, that dream haunted her.

For nights she was scared to go to sleep in case she would have another desperate dream.

During the day separate scenes from it would suddenly burst from her subconscious and blank out her mind, leaving her with a horrid, empty, big black hole at the heart of me sensation.

That dream, of the death machine, had added another half-mile of blackness to her long dark tunnel, pushing the now almost indistinguishable flicker of light even farther away.

For now she was afraid to die.

13

A HORRID NEW YEAR!

It was the last day of December, 1987. Joanna had been to a small party with some of her friends from college and was making her way home. She had been asked to be back at the family flat 'around nine', for her Dad, Elizabeth, and older brother Thomas were all going out for the evening. It would be her job to stay with her little brother Michael, junior, who was by then twelve years old.

As she walked through the brightly-lit Market Square the crowds were beginning to gather for the New Year's Eve celebrations. All these cosily-clad people were obviously in carefree mood. Balloons and streamers festooned the lamp-posts. The Cloth Hall was ablaze with twinkling coloured lights.

Pushing her way through towards that bus-stop Joanna kept asking herself, 'What is the point of all this? Tomorrow night we will be into the new year. And there will hardly be one single person out here.'

On the bus on the way home people were laughing and planning their evening. Everybody seemed so light-hearted. So cheerful. So animated.

The dejected art-student looked around with envy. In complete contrast to the excited babble all about her, she felt so heavy-hearted. So cheerless. So awful.

When she arrived back home everyone except Michael junior was almost ready to leave. He would be her company, and her charge, for the remainder of the evening.

For almost two hours after the party-goers had gone, Joanna played board games with Michael. He loved games and she was at least pleased to be able to contribute to his happiness, though searching diligently for personal satisfaction herself.

Then, after eleven o'clock, younger brother went off to bed. He was tired and totally unsentimental about 'seeing the new year in'. All he wanted to do was sleep. This left Joanna with the entire night stretching out ahead of her. And she had no intention of sleeping just yet.

When Michael had settled down for the night an eerie stillness crept over the flat. Joanna felt so alone. So isolated. So miserable. It seemed as though all the world had suddenly become involved in one big happy Game of Fun but she had been left back in the pavilion to guard their gear. Nobody loved her, she felt. Nobody wanted her, only Michael junior. And he was asleep.

To seek the solace of the presence of another human being she tiptoed into her sleeping brother's bedroom and gazed at his sleeping form. Then leaning forward she kissed him lightly on the forehead. That brought a tiny crumb of comfort to her lonely heart.

Returning to the living-room she returned to her customary pick-me-up in time of depression. Painting.

Placing a canvas on her easel she mixed some paints and began. All she wanted to use were sombre colours to reflect her mood and represent the night which had descended upon her soul.

Bold streaks of dark blue were the base colours for that painting. Unusually for her, Joanna had begun to paint, not having envisaged any particular finished product. At that moment it was important just to begin. To let her brimming heart of sadness spill over on to the canvas. To give immediate expression to her absolute dejection.

With a few broad stokes applied the canvas soon looked cold, and dark, and blue. And that image represented her mood exactly. Emotionally cold. Spiritually dark. Totally 'blue'.

On glancing at the clock to discover that it was eleven-fifty, Joanna decided that although she was alone she would celebrate the advent of the new year in the same way as she was certain hundreds of those merry makers in the Market Square would be doing. She crossed to the cupboard where she knew there was a small supply of alcohol. Then with the peculiar glow of satisfaction that comes with defiant self-assertion, like a school-boy robbing his first orchard, Joanna poured herself a glass of vodka.

Then, in two gulps, she downed half the glass. This gave her a warm glow inside. Temporarily.

Suddenly the silence of the night outside was shattered into smithereens. The blaring of horns and hooters rent the air. The bugles had been blown from the clock tower in the Market Square.

It was midnight.

A new year had begun.

Joanna sat stock still for ten minutes. She was trying to feel different. But didn't. She was trying frantically to convince herself that the new year had brought new hope. But couldn't.

Her only comfort was to return to her easel, and picking up her brush began to paint again. Slowly a picture emerged. It was a winter scene. A lake in a forest, by night. Everything about the picture was dark and forbidding. Blue-black branches of blue-black trees stood silhouetted starkly against a blue-black sky. A snow-capped mountain in the far distance added to the chilling, forbidding atmosphere.

The only light in the picture was a feeble hint of moonlight from a faint moon. The major effect of this wan moonlight was to make the surface of the lake, the shadowy forests and the bleak mountain top appear even more sinister and uninviting.

As had often been the case before, when the lonely, desolate Joanna had completed a picture she felt pleased with it. Not pleased with herself, but pleased with her work. For again she had been enabled, through her artistic escape valve, to portray the abiding anguish of her tormented soul.

Setting aside her palette, Joanna picked up her glass and had another sip of vodka, then slipped through to check on her charge, brother Michael.

He had barely budged in the bed. And was still sleeping so peacefully.

She envied him, too, not in the same way as she had envied the bus-load of babbling revellers. It was their happiness which had made her envious. Now she coveted her little brother's restful bliss.

It was three thirty in the morning. Nobody had come home.

Joanna felt forsaken.

Wandering around aimlessly seeking solace, she spied one of her most treasured books. It was a volume of poetry by John Donne, the early-seventeenth century English poet. This had been given to her as a present by one of her tutors. It had most of Donne's major works in English with Polish translations. Joanna appreciated this book so much because she loved the depth of Donne's poetry, and it also helped with her studies in English.

Curling up in an armchair she began to flick through the book. There were the favourite poems which always appealed to her. It gave a sense of security to dip into his love songs and sonnets, skim through his elegies, but it always seemed to be Donne's 'Divine Poems', as he had called them, that attracted Joanna most.

And it was at one of these that she stopped, spellbound. The words sent her mind cascading back to the dream which she had by then almost managed to forget, or at least successfully ignore. The death machine.

She read slowly, carefully, weighing every word. Could there be any solace, any succour, in poetry? In a 'Divine' poem?

> 'This is my play's last scene, here heavens appoint
> My pilgrimage's last mile; and my race
> Idly, yet quickly run, hath this last pace,
> My span's last inch, my minute's latest point,
> And gluttonous death will instantly unjoint
> My body, and soul, and I shall sleep a space …'

It was uncanny.

Joanna read that poem through three times, mesmerized.

Then she decided that she would probably shiver less in bed. She would take her book with her, though, and read herself to sleep.

Having made her final check on the sleeping Michael junior, and having given him a gentle good-night kiss, she finished what remained of the vodka, and went to bed.

It was almost five in the morning.

Later, all was silent.

Joanna's poetry book lay open where she had been reading one of the Divine Poems. The challenge of the words had gripped her, as she had read.

> 'What if this present were the world's last night?
> Mark in thy heart, O soul, where thou dost dwell,
> The picture of Christ crucified, and tell
> Whether that countenance can thee affright,
> Or tears in his eyes quench the amazing light …?

The description of the 'tears in his eyes' was touchingly topical. Joanna's eyes remained red and swollen.

There had been tears in her eyes, too.

She had cried herself to sleep.

14

LET IT FRY FOR FIVE YEARS!

With her natural aptitude for art it was to be expected that Joanna should study the subject at a more advanced level, and she did.

In September, 1988, she was enrolled as a student at the University of Fine Arts in Krakow, to study painting.

As always she enjoyed her painting. For as always, painting was her only pathway to anything even remotely resembling peace in her heart and mind. Relationships at home were becoming increasingly strained, and the deep black hole in her soul still existed. Unfilled-in. Never abating. Ever widening.

For three months Joanna made steady progress at University. It was gratifying to discover that her work was still appreciated, even on a higher, more demanding, academic plane.

Then in November she received a letter which unsettled her. It came, in a package of crayons and other art materials, from a friend in America. This woman had gone to stay for a year in USA, and thought her artistic former companion back at home would like something different to help her further her hobby and her study. Which she did.

It was the suggestion that the letter contained which served to leave the already restless Joanna even more uneasy, however. 'Would you ever consider coming out to this great country to work for a while, even a year?'

was her friend's proposal. 'You could find a job, continue your art, improve your English …'

It was an appealing proposition. A thrilling thought!

To the beleaguered mind it seemed that the end of the siege was in sight. A trip to America would afford her a sense of freedom, allow her to make lots of money, and provide her with the opportunity to both widen her experience and improve her education.

Just before Christmas when she thought his mood was right, and when she felt unusually communicative, Joanna mentioned the matter to her father.

"Mary has suggested that I should go out to see her in America for a year, dad," she began. "I would really like to go."

"And what would take you there?" Michael senior was mystified. "I can't understand what a young woman like you would want to go out there for. Anyway, sure you have just started at University. What would you do about that?"

"University would be no problem," Joanna had the answer to that one ready. "I could apply for a year off, and would probably be granted it. The universities encourage students to go abroad to improve their education. Travel is culture, they say."

Father remained unconvinced.

Although probably unwilling to admit it, and possibly even unaware of it, the mental image Michael Maciantowicz had of America had been modelled on modern movies. To him it was a country of cowboys and Indians, mobsters and gangsters, blazing guns and bows and arrows. The world of 'The Wild Bunch' and 'The Godfather'.

There was an answer to that understandable reticence, too. Defer the decision and then he will come to terms with it.

"Well I'm only considering it at this stage," Joanna replied, playing for time. "I have to apply for a visa first, and they tell me that they are very hard to get. I will apply for one and probably not be given it, so it is likely that I won't be going anyway!"

With her application sent in, Joanna stood in a line all day outside the American Embassy in Krakow, on an appointed date, to be informed of their decision. Would she be granted a visa or not? She had mixed feelings as she stood there. It would be great to be away in 'the west' but how would she cope, and would she miss Poland÷

When it came her turn, Joanna was relieved, if somewhat surprised to discover that she was to be given a visa to visit USA. Everyone in the line before her seemed to have been refused. In fact she learnt later that she was one of only three out of two hundred and fifty who had been awarded visas that day!

There was an argument to convince her father!

Although not particularly pleased at the prospect of seeing her leave Poland for a year, Michael was forced to accept it, for his determined daughter was so insistent.

All that remained for Joanna to do was to arrange for a year out from her studies. This she accomplished with relative ease, and before the end of February1989, she was on her way. From Poland, to America, to work.

On the final leg of her journey from New York to Chicago the sun was setting, and because of the elevation and direction of flight it was one of the most prolonged and most spectacular sunsets that Joanna had ever seen. The sky around outside and the interior of the cabin were all aglow in the warm orange light. That same orange light silhouetted layer upon layer of distant mountain ranges and sparkled on specks of lakes, far below.

What a contrast from the bleak and black of her New Year landscape, of more than a year before. It was the end of a day, and almost the end of a tiring journey, but Joanna wondered if perhaps it wasn't the end of an era for her, too.

Could the warmth of this sunset be the herald of brighter things to come? Tomorrow was to see the beginning of a new phase of her life.

Would it be better?

Considering how Joanna had felt over the past few years, she reckoned that it could not be any worse.

Within a few weeks she had found employment and was pleased at the thought of earning money, and huge amounts of money in comparison to what she could ever hope to earn back home. Her job was to care for a lady's mother, who had Alzheimer's Disease, while the lady herself went out to work.

It was a tiring, constant job, but Joanna was making money, gaining experience and learning the language, slowly. There were, at first, a few occasions when she found herself unable to express herself as she would have wished. That was frustrating.

It made her want to book her return ticket to Poland.

As confidence grew, and she discovered that she could make herself understood in English she began to experiment with using the language more, and then there came the times when she made fundamental mistakes in vocabulary or grammar. Other people seemed to find them funny. She found them embarrassing. They made her want to book her return ticket to Poland, too.

Like the day she undertook to explain the meal she had planned to cook for her employer and her mother that evening. It was to be beef stroganoff, and Joanna had prepared it before, for the family at home, more than once.

It was easy to cook. Well it was in Poland.

And easy to describe, too. In Polish.

Joanna began in her gradually improving but not yet perfect English.

"You cut the meat into long strips and let it fry for five years before adding the onions. That allows you time to see to the vegetables or prepare some of the other ingredients …"

The would-be-cook stopped short, for her listener appeared totally bemused. She looked like a volcano just about to erupt into rivers of laughter, but was trying to keep the cap on the crater. Either this girl thought she ate an awful lot of vegetables or else she had seriously underestimated her ability to prepare the other ingredients!

Struggling valiantly to maintain control she repeated the statement in the form of a question, "Are you sure you mean five years, Joanna?"

"Yes, five years," she insisted. "You let it fry for five years." At that her employer exploded.

"Surely you mean five minutes, dear," she corrected, gently. "I wouldn't like to eat the meat that had been fried for five years!"

Those were the times when, in the solitude of her bedroom late at night Joanna wondered to herself, 'What am I doing here? What do I want to learn this stupid language for anyway?!' And she pined for Poland. Hankered for home.

As the end of her year approached the days seem to become longer, and the sleepless nights more frequent, and even longer again.

Eventually, though, the time came to return to Krakow, and Joanna was glad for a number of reasons.

Her period of employment in America had helped her attain a number of her goals. Despite the gaffes, she had become fairly fluent in English but even more importantly the money she had earned went a long way in Poland. On arriving home in February, 1990, she was soon able to buy herself a little car in which to get around.

Now she didn't have to depend on anybody for her bus fares, any more.

She could also come and go, where and when she pleased.

That was a relief. It would stop some of the questioning and a few of the arguments at home.

Joanna now had a certain degree of independence.

But she didn't have inner peace.

America had given her much.

But it hadn't given her that.

15

THE GIRL WITH THE GOLDEN PENCIL

Having returned from her year-out to America, Joanna resumed her studies in the University of Fine Arts in Krakow, after the half-term vacation.

Immediately upon arriving back to classes she discovered that an outdoor workshop was about to begin. It was to be of two weeks duration, and was to be held at a centre in the Tatra Mountains. Here students would have the opportunity to practise their landscape painting on location.

On hearing of this workshop, Joanna was delighted. She loved landscape painting, and she loved the Tatra Mountains. A combination of both certainly sounded superb.

When they arrived at the beautiful mountain venue one of the drawing teachers announced an interesting incentive to the students, on the first morning …

"We are organising a competition, and an exhibition," he explained. "At the end of our workshop we intend to mount an exhibition in The Forum Hotel on our return to Krakow. And there will also be a drawing competition. Everyone can enter a drawing, or series of drawings, on the theme, 'Day and Night'. This work will be displayed in our own studio at the University, and the Professor and his assistant will be the judges."

Then, just before he left, to allow them to begin their work, he added, with a knowing smile, "And by the way, there is a very attractive prize for the winner."

With that the workshop began.

Many of the students set to work with a will. And why not? The air was exhilarating. The landscape was inspiring. And the prize was, the man had said, 'very attractive'.

Many of the students set to work with a will. And the many included Joanna.

However, her just back from America bubbling enthusiasm soon began to wane as she became caught up again in the slow, sleepy, lifeless atmosphere of late nights and long-lie-ins of this artistic community.

She soon began to feel discouraged, depressed and deflated, once more.

Instead of her newly-attained independence improving her inner satisfaction it had only served to increase her sense of instability. The feeling of fruitless futility and perpetual pointlessness that had plagued her person for years had returned.

There were other practical causes for her patent lack of motivation, too.

One of these was the lack of practice. The only aspect of her friend's assessment of the advantages of an American trip that did not work out for Joanna was the opportunity to continue her art. She had been so busy coping with her job, and learning the language that she had barely had time to pick up a brush!

Now she felt stale. Uninspired.

For the two weeks of that course she performed under par. She viewed the breath-taking scenery, took some photographs, made some sketches, did some paintings, but nothing pleased her.

It was not her best work, and Joanna knew that it was not her best work, but she was so dispirited that she found herself incapable of caring.

When she arrived back home, late on the Friday evening at the end of the workshop, however, Joanna thought, 'Day and night. I must submit something for this competition.'

Slowly, but surely the inspiration returned. And as she looked at one of the photographs she had taken on her trip an idea began to develop in her mind.

Day and night. Day was where she lived. And night was how she felt.

Day was light and bright. Night crept in at the death of day.

The only chance of cheer in a night, was to add a light, to make it bright …

Placing a sheet of paper on an easel Joanna picked up a stick of charcoal and began to draw a scene suggested by her photograph. By day.

It was a picture of high steep mountains rising into jagged peaks which pierced the sky. The lower slopes of the mountains were covered with trees, of various shapes.

The only sign of human involvement in the otherwise unspoiled landscape was the railway line. This line emerged from a black hole, a tunnel mouth, at the left of the picture and hugged the side of the rocky slopes, disappearing and reappearing amongst clumps of trees, until it eventually went out of the picture, around the back of a hill to the right.

In the foreground of the picture there was a valley floor with a shining stream threading its way around a series of boulders and rocky outcrops. A few sheep grazed on what grass they could find. An old man with a crook and his sheepdog were walking up into the scene, from the bottom right hand corner.

Although executed in charcoal, the final drawing, when Joanna was satisfied that she had represented the landscape of her original photograph accurately, gave the impression of a very pleasing, peaceful panorama.

It was obviously daytime, for every detail of the tranquil mountain vista attracted the eye, inviting inspection.

The sense of achievement to be able, eventually, to produce a piece of work that pleased her once more, spurred Joanna on, throughout the weekend, to complete the second part of her unfolding plan.

Her next drawing was of the same place, but at a different time.

In number two the mountains were solemn shadows of shape, blocks of black, against a sky rendered sombre by broad streaks of charcoal. Almost every other aspect of the detail of the former picture was lost in vague indefinable outline. There was no shepherd, and no sheepdog. The valley floor was covered by black blobs which could have been rocks, or sheep, or almost anything else.

The myriad of trees on the mountain slopes were one large murky mass.

This picture, however, contained a contrast, which was absent from the earlier, peaceful daytime picture. For from the tunnel to the left of the drawing the front of a train had just appeared. The stunning, and immediately arresting feature of this latest drawing was the light from the front of the train. The only intrusion of any other colour on to that scene, other than the black of the charcoal, was the inclusion of a startling shaft of bright yellow light piercing the surrounding darkness from a single lamp mounted high up on the front of the silhouetted steam engine. It cut a swathe of light through the surrounding gloom.

When she had finished that second picture Joanna felt even more satisfied. Now, for her, the contrast was complete. With the aid of some charcoal she had managed to portray the distinction between day and night, and with one simple stroke of a yellow crayon, she had symbolized her quest for happiness. Out of the blackness of the tunnel there shone a ray of light which illuminated the way ahead, dispelling all the darkness in its path.

That was what she was desperately craving. The light to dispel her darkness. Light at the far end of her tunnel of guilt and fear, of emptiness and loneliness, of malice and mistrust.

Her duo of complementary yet contrasting drawings meant something to her. They said something important to her, for her, and about her. But would they mean anything to anyone else?

Next week, and the competition, would be the test.

On Monday back at University all the students who had been on the two-week workshop in the Tatra Mountains submitted their work for display in the exhibition, and also their competition entry. 'Day and night.'

The University staff were going to judge the exhibition and the Professor and his assistant would require time to make their decision. Those entering the competition had been asked not to sign their drawings so that the judges could not be influenced by their know ledge of the students' previous work. Since students at all levels had been invited to enter, the results of the competition would be announced after classes next day, Tuesday.

That afternoon a subdued, but secretly hopeful, group of students assembled in the studio where the exhibition had been staged.

When she walked in and surveyed the work on display Joanna reckoned that she had little chance of competing against such opposition. Some of the work was brilliant, she thought. Yet up on the back wall her striking streak of yellow light seemed to blaze out from the blackness of her drawing. Perhaps it was a sign of hope.

When the Professor came to announce the results he kept everybody on tenterhooks for ages, telling the competitors things they already knew. He went on and on about the dedication of the staff, the extremely high standard of work, the obvious hours spent in preparation for the competition ... And all the crowd of students wanted to know was who had won!

Eventually, the result, they had all been waiting for came.

"We have decided, after much deliberation, to award first prize to the pair of charcoal drawings on the back wall," he announced. Then, looking round over the expectant audience he went on to enquire, "Does anyone know whose it is?"

Although the judges did not know who had done the drawings, many of the other students did. And many heads turned, like clockwork, in Joanna's direction.

Conscious of the gaze of so many eyes upon her, she stood up. Stiffly. Shyly.

Stiffly because she had been sitting for so long.

Shyly, because she was embarrassed at being the centre of attention.

"Please come forward and receive your prize, Joanna," the Professor went on to invite, smiling down to where she was standing, looking extremely self-conscious, in the second row.

A cheer rose when Joanna went forward. All her fellow-students were gifted artists themselves and well able to recognise artistic excellence when they encountered it.

Joanna received her prize, and murmured her thanks.

On returning to her seat she opened the package to discover that it was, as had been promised, 'a very attractive prize'.

It was a beautiful golden pencil.

Before leaving the exhibition hall, Joanna returned to her drawings. For one last look. Other students were standing around, discussing them, analysing them, trying to interpret them.

Joanna smiled. Some of them were way off the mark. Only she knew what they meant. And she was more convinced than ever that there was an answer to her misery, a remedy for her soul-sickness, a light at the end of her tunnel of darkness.

She would find it.

She must find it.

Somehow. Somewhere. And soon!

16

THE LAND OF THE RISING SUN

During the next few months life at home became most unpleasant. Joanna became even more resentful of any kind of rule or authority from anybody, including the rules and regulations, as she saw them, of the Church. So she stopped attending Mass completely. She was even more determined that she could make her own way in life. Nobody was ever going to compel her to conform to any preconceived pattern!

She had been independent in America. And she could assert her independence in Poland, too.

During the early part of that year Joanna joined some of the other students in exploring yet another avenue in her attempt to run away from reality. Establish her identity. Discover real peace. She began to meet them in the Planty, the beautiful border of trees surrounding Krakow's city centre, to experiment with smoking marijuana.

This afforded another experience, which the almost distraught art student hoped would prize open an escape hatch into freedom and fulfilment. But it didn't. It merely amounted to another failed attempt. There was a 'No Exit' sign at the other end of that avenue. It was just another cul-de-sac of disappointment. The only way out was back.

Marijuana was not the answer.

At Easter, Joanna refused to spend the holiday with the family. Everyone else was spending the weekend together and they expected that she would be joining them, as she had previously always done. This time, however, she stated categorically that she would not be joining them. Refused point blank to even consider it.

This caused bad feeling to grow worse at home.

Sullen resentment deteriorated into outright rancour.

Joanna yelled at one point, "No! I am not staying in here with you all weekend! And if I could find anywhere else to live I wouldn't be living here either!" The twenty-one year old young woman had worked herself into such a state of animosity that all she wanted to do was break out, and stay out. Break free and feel free. Break away and stay away.

Her overall craving was for peace in her heart. But where was that to be found?

She was turning her own life, and every body else's too, it seemed, both inside out and upside down in a turmoil of searching, and as yet she had not found the answer.

Then one day, just out of the blue, she thought she had solved the problem. As she was passing a travel agency, on one of her city centre aimless wanderings, late one May afternoon, she noticed a sign in the window. It was extolling the virtues and attractions of Japan, the Land of the Rising Sun.

For some reason Joanna found that advert particularly appealing, and the prospect of a trip to the Orient extremely alluring. The fare would not present the same problem to her as it would to many others, either, for she was still drawing on her American reserve.

Fired up with the idea of spending the summer away from home, Joanna spoke to Mary, who had been with her in America and was pleased to find that she would be thrilled to make the trip with her. She, too, relished the prospect of a summer out of Poland.

After a month of preparation, in early July Joanna and her friend Mary set off for Japan.

Two years previously Joanna had travelled as far west as she had imagined it possible to go. To America. Now she was travelling as far east as she imagined it possible to go. To Japan.

Her experiences in America had broadened her outlook, but hadn't calmed her restless spirit. They had enhanced her education without satisfying her seeking soul.

What would Japan, the Land of the Rising Sun, have to offer? Would it prove to be the land of the new dawn? The new dawn at the start of a clearer, brighter day?

It proved to be an interesting summer. Joanna enjoyed learning all she could about a new and totally different culture. Being an artist meant that she could focus particularly on the art in any society, and she was happy to do this in Japan. The only thing she could never learn was the language. She reckoned that it would take her a lot longer than the six weeks she had to spare, or indeed the year she had spent in America, to learn Japanese!

Possibly the incident which had more of a lasting impact on her than anything else that she either learnt or experienced on her trip to the Far East was the afternoon in which she, Mary, and another student friend whom they had met on their travels, and who spoke Japanese, were walking through the gardens of a Buddhist temple.

It was a beautiful day. The sun shone from cloudless blue. The still air was filled with the scent of flowers. Banks and splashes of colour from the blooms of the flowers and the leaves of the shrubs and trees merged into a picture, in whichever direction one looked.

The three young women were walking around at leisurely pace, soaking up every possible aspect of the enchanting scene, when they noticed a Japanese monk approaching them.

This man was dressed in long white flowing robes with voluminous sleeves. He carried a string of brilliantly coloured beads loosely between his two hands. These he kept moving easily between deft fingers. The beads attracted Joanna. How she would love a string of them!

As he came close to the foreign visitors, the monk slackened his pace. When they met he had slowed almost to a stop. It was obvious that he wished to welcome these tourists to his temple but was at a loss to know how to address them. He didn't even know what country they had come from, or what language they spoke.

Anxious to save him any embarrassment, the Japanese speaker greeted him with a simple, 'Good afternoon'.

At once the small man in white appeared very pleased and gave them a very warm welcome to his country, and to that particular temple. Then, much to the surprise of the three visitors, he invited them to accompany him to the tea garden.

When they had, through their interpreter, accepted his invitation, the monk set off to lead the way, his pace having quickened, his beads now held tightly, and the sleeves of his robe billowing out at either side.

As they walked briskly behind him, the girl who spoke Japanese and had studied the customs of the country for four years in University, said with an air of consternation, "I just cannot believe this is happening. Normally strangers are never allowed into the tea garden. It is usually just followers of the Buddhist religion who go in there."

If the outer garden was beautiful the tea garden was nothing short of magnificent!

In true Japanese tradition the three visitors were invited to sit cross legged on a bamboo mat on the floor. When they had duly seated themselves in time-honoured fashion the visitors found that they were on a wide verandah, and directly opposite them was a most imposing golden palace, whose shining towers, resplendent in the sunshine reminded Joanna of the golden dome on Wawel Cathedral back in her home city. In Krakow, however, there was one golden dome. Here there seemed to be dozens, all elaborately designed and exquisitely crafted.

Between the shining palace and their shady verandah there was a lake, and the towers and turrets of the palace were perfectly reflected in its mirror-like surface. Huge blue and yellow dragon-flies, as big as baby birds, flitting between the huge, almost artificial-looking in their perfection, pink and white water-lilies, helped to contribute to the overall tranquility of the scene.

Joanna, the artist, was almost overawed.

Soon the tea was brought and as the trio sat sipping it from the flat bowls in which it was served, the monk began telling them through their Japanese interpreter about the temple, about his religion, and particularly about his god, Buddha.

This man was so fervent in the following of his faith, and the whole setting was one of such undisturbed calm, that Joanna made up her mind about something sitting there.

If this religion could produce such peace in its followers she would find out more about it when she arrived home, from somebody who could tell her something about it in her own language.

And there was a Buddhist temple in Krakow.

She knew that.

17

LEGS OF STONE

Within months of her return from Japan in late summer, Joanna did two things she had been planning for some time. One was the promise to herself, made that idyllic day in the Buddhist temple tea garden, to further investigate the focus of Oriental religions. The second, was the practical enactment of what had begun more as a threat than a promise, five months before.

With her enquiring mind and spiritually void and hungry soul she began her task of investigation enthusiastically. Perhaps the answer to all her problems was to be found somewhere in these strange Eastern beliefs and patterns of worship. She would certainly see.

For months she searched, asking many questions, reading many books.

After some study, and in line with the teaching of some of these 'faiths', Joanna became a vegetarian, stopping eating meat of all sorts, completely. Then, in the further belief that her spiritual state was in some way related to her physical well-being she began to frequent the canteen attached to the Buddhist temple in Krakow, to eat only their specially prepared food.

As she talked to other students about these things, she soon discovered that some of them believed that their future was 'in the stars'. So for a period Joanna immersed herself in astrology. Then she heard of another person who claimed to be able to foretell the future 'from the cards'. So she then proceeded to experiment with Tarot cards. Then, soon after that she was present at a series of seances.

If she could only contact the world of spirits, or know something about the future, or discover anything significant about the spiritual realm that she knew existed outside her own body and being, it would perhaps help her to take her first steps on the road to happiness.

This was a period of intense mental and spiritual anguish for Joanna. Although unaware of it at the time she was careering blindly on into even bleaker blackness.

The torment of the increasingly frantic but frustratingly futile quest for inner rest was further exacerbated by the emotional wrench of pulling out of the family flat into her own studio. Before the start of the new term Joanna had rented a city centre apartment in the shadow of the historic Wawel Castle. To her this should have brought some relief, for now she had a place in which she could both live and work, without the external pressures of family demands and expectations.

It didn't work that way, though, for although she was free to come and go as she pleased, during the dark winter days, Joanna was still afflicted by the internal agony of her own personal pursuit of permanent peace.

Before Christmas she stopped attending most of her lectures at University. What is the point in going there? She reasoned. The only thing left in all of the world from which she derived just the tiniest hint of satisfaction was her painting. And she could do that at home. At least when she was working in her own studio she was alone with her own thoughts and in her own turmoil. She wasn't compelled to listen to self-opinionated people making self-originated points on totally trivial topics.

There didn't seem to be any meaning to life anyway, so why should she have to associate with anybody, even those who thought they were somebody, any more?

For weeks she shut herself off from the outside world, doing nothing but painting, and leaving her studio just once a day to scurry out to the Buddhist canteen for a vegetarian meal. Other than that she barely ate and seldom slept.

When her teachers enquired about her absence she assured them that although she was not attending their classes she was continuing to paint. When she showed them some of the art work she had produced in her pain they were impressed. Thus, appreciating that their talented student was in a very unstable state of mind, they came to an agreement.

Joanna was to attend University at least once a month, with a stipulated quota of work. Otherwise she was free to work on her own. In her own studio. At her own speed.

Early in the new year she heard of something which she thought would be interesting, possibly even stimulating. It would probably be too much to expect, though, in her distressed state of mind, that it would be satisfying. But at least it offered yet another faint flicker of hope.

Although now despairing of ever finding rest, Joanna was still prepared to clutch at spiritual straws.

On a Saturday in February a massive Buddhist rally was to be held in a conference centre in her home city. A celebrated master from Denmark was coming to conduct this rally. This, according to the advertising material, was a significant coup for Krakow.

During her earlier research into the subject Joanna had learnt that in the Buddhist religion there was a number of 'masters' any one of whose teachings an adherent could follow. How many times had she not concluded, during those aimless, fruitless, trying-everything-but-satisfied-with-nothing days, that what she needed was a 'master' to follow? Somebody who would inject both purpose and direction into her life.

The prospect of attending that rally give her a forward focus until the date of it came around. In her self-imposed seclusion she even began to dare to hope for happiness. Perhaps this eminent 'master' could strike the elusive match to set the light at the end of her dark tunnel blazing forth in all its glory.

On the day of the rally the conference centre was crowded. Since nobody sat on chairs, and chairs took up space, many more people could be packed into the available space.

By the time Joanna arrived it seemed that there were hundreds of people sitting cross-legged on mats on the floor, waiting.

She found herself a space on a mat, and joined the others, waiting.

Just before the rally was due to begin hundreds more had crammed into the centre and had found themselves spaces on mats, and joined the others, waiting.

Before the guest 'master' came on stage almost six hundred people were seated on every possible spot on the floor, waiting.

The eventual appearance of the long-awaited speaker was greeted with muted, respectful applause. He was an imposing figure. His white hair and all-white attire, top, trousers and shoes, gave the impression of light and right.

And light and right were what Joanna had come to find.

The single distinctive, and almost incongruent, item of the 'master's' dress was the coloured plaited cord around his neck, on which was suspended a dark turquoise stone.

For over an hour the Danish teacher outlined the 'wisdom' of Buddhism, extolling its worth. As he came towards the end of his address he seemed to repeat, with increasing frequency, that anyone restless or troubled could take refuge, and find rest in that religion. He assured his audience that if they embraced Buddhism, the good spirits would live with them and take care of them for the remainder of their lives. They would be assigned to a master, who would lead them to solve any, or all, of their problems.

The rally ended with an invitation.

Anyone who wished to accepted the Buddhist faith, with all its alleged attendant benefits for life and living, was asked to come up to the front and be blessed by 'the master'.

Many in the rapt audience needed no second call.

At once people from all over the huge hall, began to rise to their feet like plants sprouting from fertile soil, and move in a steady stream towards the platform.

Still seated, Joanna watched with keen interest to see what would happen next.

And it was fascinating. Absolutely absorbing.

One by one the would-be devotees to Buddhism stood before the master, and one-by-one he placed his hand upon their shoulder, and then the top of their head. Following this he lifted the dark stone on the gold chain, and with the stone he touched the forehead of every person as they passed, muttering a few words as he did so.

There then began yet another struggle in a mind that was no stranger to struggles. The mind of Joanna Maciantowicz.

Perhaps this is the answer, she reasoned. At last I have found the source of comfort that will end my inner cravings. All these people appear so happy. And they will have the good spirits to protect them and the teachings of a master to guide them for the remainder of their lives.

This is what I will do. I will get up when the line grows shorter and there is room for me at the front, and I will go forward to be blessed by the master.

And it was then that a most incredible thing happened.

Having determined to go forward, at an appropriate time, Joanna chose what she thought would be the right time when the pressure on the platform had eased a bit, and tried to rise to make her way forward, but couldn't!

No matter how hard she tried, she couldn't move. It was a strange, almost sinister, sensation. It felt as though a huge and powerful hand was placing irresistible pressure on the top of her head, and on her shoulders, pushing her down into, and almost through, her mat. And her legs, which had been crossed for so long were now locked together, and refused to move. They had become extremely heavy and totally motionless, as though carved in marble, or made of stone.

Joanna could not move.

For more than a minute she tried in vain to rise, but her legs would not work. No matter how hard she tried she could not make them budge even an inch! Nor could she overcome the pressing power on her head and shoulders, the parts of her body which 'the master' would have touched.

Then, just after the last person had crossed the platform at the front and the master had disappeared behind the stage curtains, the unseen pressure eased and her pins and needles legs moved stiffly. But at least they moved.

What a relief!

For a few terrifying moments Joanna had begun to panic, believing that she had suddenly been afflicted by some dreadful, incurable, crippling disease.

As she left the conference centre later, in the middle of a chattering crowd, she was solitary and silent, still in a state of shock.

She had, however, begun to have her doubts.

Did Buddhism hold the key?

Was this the solution to her situation?

Was this the light at the end of her tunnel of darkness?

Or was it somewhere else?

18

ANGEL FACE

After the summer vacation in 1992 Joanna began to return more regularly to University for two reasons, both of which were related to new subjects which had been introduced to her course for that year. One of these was a philosophical discipline called 'The Theory of Culture' and the other an attractive subject to Joanna, entitled 'Architectural Painting'.

Although she was still both spiritually seeking and emotionally empty, and all she really wanted to do was set herself apart and paint, Joanna found the prospect of immersing herself in The Theory of Culture an inviting intellectual challenge.

And the second reason for her slightly more regular return was a project in Architectural Painting which was immediately appealing to the gifted artist.

The governing body of the University of Fine Arts decided that it would be an appropriate statement of the ethos of their institution, and an adequate acknowledgment of the aptitude of their students, if they had them design and paint a large mural in the hallway of one of the college buildings. Recognising that having her personally involved could yield a number of benefits, the Professor in charge of the project invited Joanna to be one of the artists responsible.

During the autumn months, and into the draughty winter days in the hallway, Joanna and the others muralists painted and talked, both with each other and with the host of others who stopped to cast a critical eye over their maturing masterpiece.

The conversations were not all confined to artistic concerns, however. Topics covered could range from sport to science, from dress to drama, from coffee to culture. From anything to everything.

There were occasional times though, when the discussions, skilfully manipulated by the still joyless Joanna, turned to what had become her sole obsession ...

The longing for light. The pursuit of peace. Fullness for emptiness. Happiness for hopelessness.

There was one girl, Joanna noticed, who whenever such subjects were under the spotlight, invariably introduced a different angle from anybody else. Isa, as she was called, kept talking about things like sin and guilt, about the love of God and the death of Christ. And also the Holy Spirit.

Here He was again, this Holy Spirit, that Majka had mentioned with such warmth and enthusiasm during those blessings-at-breakfast Dominican days.

What she could not fail but note about this particular student was the fact that she seemed to speak of these matters, not in a cold and calculating, remote and reasoned fashion, but with exactly the same warmth and enthusiasm which had been the magic of Majka.

She was full of it the girl! From head to toe. It was bubbling up in her and then bursting out.

Isa's secret seemed to be that she not only knew what she was talking about, but she actually lived what she was talking about!

As the winter wore on and the painting progressed there was something else Joanna observed about this particular girl as well.

Over the weeks and months she had spent standing on steps in that hallway, usually with a bunch of brushes in her hand, she had remarked that this eager and sincere student was one of a group of five or six who occasionally disappeared through a door into a small room opposite the mural. It usually happened at lunch time or late in the afternoon after lectures. The people who went in there, singly and in silence generally emerged, about half an hour later, in an animated group, engaged in lively conversation.

In addition to Isa, whose fire and fervour impressed her, Joanna knew all the other students who periodically disappeared behind that door.

Mariola, Peter and Martin seemed to be with Isa every time. Others came occasionally.

Just before Christmas Joanna had to change studio. She had to leave the one she had been renting near Wawel Castle because the lady owner had died so she moved out to an apartment farther out of the city centre, and totally unaware of at the time, on the same bus route as Martin used to travel out to where he lived.

One dark, wet, winter evening Joanna and Martin were travelling back from University on the same bus, and they were sitting together.

Joanna had been waiting for an opportunity like this for quite some time.

She had always been anxious to know what it was that he and his friends did behind that closed door but had never been able to find out.

This was her chance.

When they had settled themselves in their soaking clothes on the already-soaking seat, and exchanged observations about the dreadful day, Joanna went straight to the point. Time was not on her side. She only had seven stops to solve the mystery of the disappearing students.

"I hope you don't mind me asking, Martin," she began, "but I have seen you and some others going into that little room off the main hallway a number of times. What do you go in there for?"

Martin smiled in a very special way.

It was not an ideal day for seeing angels. The rain on the outside of the bus window was being chased down the panes by the condensation on the inside. Everyone around looked wet and woebegone.

But with the combination of the soft lights in the bus, and the rain-filtered rays of a street lamp they were just passing, resting on Martin's face, it seemed, just for the moment of that special smile, that his face shone like the face of an angel.

It appeared to Joanna that he was just in that fleeting instant, transfigured. He looked not like Martin the art student, but like some sort of heavenly messenger.

There was a radiance in his smile which she had never seen in a human being before. Was this the light at the end of the tunnel?

Martin the messenger didn't answer the question immediately. Rather he opened his overcoat and began to fumble in one of the inner pockets for something.

'What is he going to produce from way in there?' The entranced enquirer wondered.

That query did not take long to resolve.

Fondly, graciously, reverently, as though he had just been privileged to handle some priceless work of art, Martin pulled from an inner pocket, a small black book.

This little book he held loosely on his knee so that the pages flicked open, and over. Looking down at it Joanna could see that in many parts it had been underlined or highlighted in a range of different colours. These, she concluded, must be the parts of this book that are of particular importance. Her book of Donne's poetry was all marked.

Observing her keen interest in his book, he went on to give her the answer she had been seeking for so long.

"This," Martin explained, "is my Bible. When we go into that room you are talking about, we go in there to study the Bible. And to pray.'

"To study the Bible?" Joanna repeated the words. "Why do you want to study the Bible? Why is it so important to you? Why not just study poetry? Or even other religions?"

Martin smiled again. His face glowed again.

He understood her confusion.

"We study the Bible because we believe that it contains God's plan for the salvation of mankind. In fact we believe it to be the Living Word of God," he went on patiently to explain.

Suddenly, in a crowded steamed-up bus, Joanna's mind flashed back to the morning in the Dominican Church when she had first come across the phrase, 'Living Word.'

It had been in a chorus that had gripped her imagination. And for the intervening turbulent years she had forgotten all about that morning. She had long since forgotten too, her fervent request at that particular time.

'Please let the Living Word, whoever or whatever it is, speak to me,' had been her impassioned plea.

It all came flooding back.

"I would like to hear more about this, Martin," Joanna went on, quietly.

"Don't worry, you will," Martin assured her, rising, and smiling again. "But I have to get off here. This is my stop. I will talk to you about this any time. Sometime soon, if you like."

With that he turned and had just time to hear Joanna's whispered, "That would be good," before disappearing down the bus, off the bus, and into the murk of a winter evening.

Joanna had to travel on for one more stop. She sat there, almost in a trance.

She felt that for a split second she had seen the face of an angel.

She felt that at last she had finger-tip-touched the truth. Again.

The light at the end of her tunnel of darkness had spluttered into life. Again.

19

THAT'S 'A'

Throughout that year at University Joanna found her studies in 'The Theory Of Culture' to be a stimulating experience for her endlessly enquiring mind.

This was a nebulous, non-examination subject designed to widen students' perspectives on such abstract values as life and living, success and society, environment and education. This course was to be assessed on a thesis to be submitted by each student at the end of the academic year.

Since each person was encouraged to select his or her own theme for the thesis, subject to college approval, Joanna undertook to delve into the vast topic, 'The Meaning Of Life'.

This choice of subject afforded her the opportunity to consider in detail the question that she had often asked herself during those difficult growing-older and growing-darker days of teenage.

Why do I feel the way I do? What am I here for anyway?

As her university career progressed Joanna had begun to be ever more specific about her feelings. Her perpetual inner query had now advanced from the more general 'Why do I feel the way I do?' to the more definitive,

'Why am I so singularly unhappy all the time?'

'Why,' she kept asking herself, 'does life ahead just appear as one long, lightless, cheerless, hopeless tunnel?'

Joanna looked a lonely figure in the University library on a number of occasions. She often sat until closing time poring over ponderous tomes. All in the hunt for answers. In the search for satisfaction.

There would be no book left unread, no stone left unturned, no lamp left unlit, in her pursuit of permanent peace.

Conscious that she would be required to attend a consultation with her tutor in mid-February, 1993, to outline progress on the project so far, Joanna jotted down the drift of her deliberations. This was not intended to be by any means the finished product, but through a series of questions and definitions she had begun to determine the direction her study was to take.

It was to her, the artist, the outline sketch to which the finer details of colour tone and texture were waiting to be added.

It was the skeleton, lacking both flesh and features. It was basic. But it was a start.

'What is happiness?' she began.

'The feeling of happiness is usually the result of an inner stimulus or an outward influence.'

According to an ancient theory in one of the many huge books she consulted happiness was 'a state of perfection which a man can achieve by his own strength or power.'

This was confusing. Joanna jotted down her immediate reaction. That assertion had catapulted her into an instant state of self-examination.

'Do I have enough strength? Or enough power? No. I don't think so.'

Then she added somewhat cynically, 'Even if I did have enough power, which I don't, what would I do with it to bring me happiness? How would I use it?'

Yet another definition of 'happiness' which she discovered in her quest for 'The Meaning of Life', was, 'happiness in the recognition and realisation of goodness'.

That set her ship of tortured thought sailing off on another tack.

'If happiness is the recognition and realisation of goodness, what then is 'goodness'?'

Thoughts poured out as Joanna pursued the subject of goodness. 'And surely what is good for one person is not good for another,' she began. 'And if this is true, how then am I to recognise and realise goodness if I cannot determine my own particular strain of goodness?'

After many more jottings, spread loosely over many pages, Joanna came to the conclusion that to identify goodness there must be some base, some benchmark, some universally accepted yardstick for it.

That feature she assumed to be the moral law.

The introduction of a moral law into her argument presented the digging herself in ever deeper anxious researcher with another dilemma. If a moral law establishes a standard of goodness, are all those who either fail to come up to the stipulated standard or break the recognized rules, by inference, evil?

Socrates, she discovered, contended that 'a man always has goodness before his eyes, but it is lack of knowledge, not lack of virtue, that prevents him from achieving his goal.' Education would improve everything.

That theory Joanna dismissed out of hand.

She was as well educated as most in Krakow, and she was sure she felt more miserable than most in Krakow.

Knowledge was not a generator of goodness.

'Is it then a question of values?' she wrote in her notes.

'Is goodness the choosing of higher values? The keeping of a moral law, and imposed code of conduct?

'And is evil, by contrast, the settling for lower values? Ignoring the moral law and its imposed code of conduct?

'If that is the case, why is it that even when I resolve to chose the higher values, to behave in accordance with the accepted moral law, I still find myself being drawn, inexorably, by some unseen force, to settle for the lower values?

'Why can I not just simply attain to goodness?

'And then ultimately achieve happiness through goodness?'

Questions, questions, questions …

Something she had read about Christianity seemed to ha answer to one of those questions.

After perusing as many articles as she could find on what Christian religion taught on the subject she was intrigued to discover that 'a knowledge of the right and the good' was not enough.

Joanna continued to advance her arguments, simultaneously airing her inner afflictions, on yet more sheets of paper.

'No matter how hard we try to do good, or attain to goodness, it seems that we cannot', she reflected, 'because our nature is not intrinsically good, but intrinsically evil. Christianity has a word for this inclination to evil. It calls it sin.'

Reverting to the work of her favourite poet, Joanna was able to illustrate this point.

'The English poet John Donne explains his problem with this inborn propensity to evil in the following poem. Then, in her own handwriting she scribbled it out in its entirety …

'A Hymn To God The Father'
Wilt thou forgive my sin, where I begun,
Which is my sin, though it were done before?
Wilt thou forgive those sins through which I run
And do them still, though still I do deplore?
When thou hast done, thou hast not done,
For I have more.

Wilt thou forgive that sin, by which I have won
Others to sin, and made my sin their door?
Wilt thou forgive that sin which I did shun'
A year or two, but wallowed in a score?
When thou hast done, thou hast not done,
For I have more.

I have a sin of fear that when I have spun
My last thread, I shall perish on the shore;
Swear by thy self that at my death, thy Son
Shall shine as he shines now, and heretofore;
And having done that, thou hast done,
I have no more.

The poet's problem is mine.

'those sins through which I run,
And do them still, though still I do deplore'

Why do people have to spend their whole lives afflicted with this disposition towards sin? Why can they not just live in an undisturbed state of goodness and happiness? Would it not make life more pleasant for everyone on the planet if it was like that?

That was all of her dissertation outline she had completed before attending her mid-session meeting with her teacher.

So she printed across the bottom of her final-page-so-far, TO BE CONTINUED ...

Next afternoon she sat wondering what her supervising lecturer was thinking as he read her notes and observations. She had no definite indication whatsoever. It was impossible to make sense of a slow nod of the head, the hint of a grin, or briefly raised eyebrows.

He had only been sifting through the pile of pages for five minutes before making any recognisable response. To the waiting, wondering Joanna, though, it seemed like five hours.

With the air of one satisfied-without-saying-it he placed Joanna's by now untidy looking sheaf of notes on the desk in front of him and for the next ten minutes he discussed the arguments, assertions and assumptions in them with her.

As he drew their discussion to a close the university teacher handed Joanna's notes back to her with a broad smile and the comment, "I don't think I will be needing to see you again Joanna. That's 'A'!"

Ten minutes later Joanna was walking down the broad stone steps and out of the building, into the gathering dusk of a winter evening. It was only half-way through the academic year and she had been awarded an 'A' in one of her subjects.

She should have been delighted. But she wasn't.

Her series of reasoned observations had been 'A' to a philosopher.

But to her they were more like 'C'. For Confusion.

Or perhaps even just 'D'. For Desperation.

For now she had identified her problem. Her darkness, her disillusionment, her despair, were all a result of her inborn inability to be good. Her natural inclination to evil.

Sin, as some Christians called it.

Her great dilemma now was that she had identified the problem, but could not find any solution to it.

She had kept digging and digging into philosophical thought until she had dug herself into a huge hole from which there seemed to be no way out.

Lying in bed that night, Joanna was unable to sleep, so she switched on the bedside light, and scribbled in her diary which she always kept beside

her, 'Somewhere far, far away and deep, deep down inside my inner space
I hear this awful scream. No silence. No inner peace.'

Joanna was faced with a stark choice.

She either had to find answers soon. Or stop digging.

For she was on the verge of mental melt-down.

20

THE ONE BOOK MAN AND
THE MANIC BOOKWORM

On certain evenings that winter, Joanna had found herself on the same bus home as Martin, the man with the well-marked Bible.

Occasionally, if they could find a seat beside each other Joanna would ask him about the Bible studies back in University, and he was always willing to answer all her questions.

The more she talked to this young man, the more Joanna realised that there was something different about him. Martin always seemed so serene. What she particularly liked about him, too, was that he could appear so sincere and sympathetic without being sanctimonious.

After a number of casual on the way home discussions Joanna gradually became aware of something else. On that first night when he had referred to his Bible as the 'Living Word of God' she had caught the first faint and feeble flickerings of it. Now she had become absolutely convinced of it.

However he had it, or wherever he had it, or why ever he had it, she did not know, but Martin had the light at the end of her tunnel of darkness.

One evening she extended an invitation to him.

It was an idea she had been contemplating for some time, and the more she thought of it the more she became convinced that it was the proper course of action. She had also concluded that it now represented her only hope of achieving anything even slightly resembling soul satisfaction.

"I am at present writing a dissertation on 'The Meaning of Life' for my Theory of Culture class, Martin," she began one evening, "and I was wondering if you could come round to my apartment sometime and tell me what Christianity and the Bible have to say about it. All I know is that it is something about sin. But there must be more to it than that."

"Yes, Joanna," Martin replied, immediately acutely aware that there was more to this request than a call for help with a philosophical project. It was the cry of a hungry heart. "There is much more to it than that. I will come round any night and talk to you about it. What night suits?"

Before Martin left the bus a night acceptable to both was found, and a meeting arranged.

As she travelled on her one more stop Joanna felt that she was making progress.

Perhaps now she would find some answers to her endless questions about happiness and goodness, about loneliness and emptiness, about sin and its solution, from Martin. He seemed to know what he was talking about, at least.

When the pre-arranged Tuesday night came around Martin arrived at Joanna's door at seven-thirty. He had nothing with him but his Bible.

What a contrast, though, when Joanna showed her guest into the living-room of her new studio. The shiny antique table was covered with large volumes on philosophy. On psychology. On religion. On oriental cults.

After a few preliminary pleasantries, Martin took a seat at one side of the table, and Joanna sat down opposite him, behind her barricade of books.

"What's your problem, Joanna?" Martin enquired, amiably. He thought he had a fair idea of what was unsettling his fellow art student. But it would be helpful to hear her own perception of it.

"My problem is my constant unhappiness. And the cause of my constant unhappiness," came the instant and honest reply. "I have been reading all these books," and with a sweep of her hand she embraced them all, "but I can find no answers. I understand that Christianity says there is something called sin. If everybody has sin does that mean that everybody is bad? And therefore nobody can possibly be happy?"

Martin sat in silence for a moment.

He had been briefly taken aback by the candour of that opening cascade of confusion.

"Yes, and no." The beginning of Martin's response didn't sound too promising.

"I say 'Yes', because I believe that the basic problem afflicting mankind is sin," he continued, "but 'No' to your other question. That does not mean that nobody can possibly be happy any more."

Joanna was fascinated by this approach. She wanted to hear his reasons for these assertions. And said so.

"You will need to explain that a bit more," she went on. "Yes," Martin was patient. "I intend to do that."

Then for the next ten minutes he outlined to his hostess some instances from his own experience. Some of these Joanna already knew about, but most of them she didn't.

He told her how that he had once been like her, seeking for peace, dabbling in the occult. That was the bit Joanna knew about, for on a student painting trip to Prague, Martin had been a leader in a series of all night spiritist seances.

What she had been totally unaware of was the more recent transformation in his life, and how it had occurred. Martin went on to tell her about it. He explained how that he, like her, had become disillusioned and how that once he had heard about how that Jesus Christ had come to earth to die on a cross to take away his sin ... and how that he had believed this... and how that now he had been released from this bondage to sin ... and how that he was happy in his new faith.

There could be no denying his final claim.

He certainly looked, and sounded, happy in his new faith.

It was the other things he said that confused Joanna.

"You mean to tell me," she responded eventually, after musing on Martin's message for a few minutes, "That every single person in this world is in sin?"

"Yes," Martin said, "That's right." Then leafing through his little Bible he found the page he had obviously been looking for and then continued, "It says here, 'For all have sinned and come short of the glory of God'".

Although initially unwilling to admit it, that was the way Joanna felt. She knew that she felt empty, she was missing some vital ingredient in her life, she was falling short of something, but hadn't ever entertained the notion that it was 'the glory of God'.

Loath to accept this rather sweeping statement from Martin's little black book as definitive truth, Joanna resorted to hypothesis.

"Just suppose then for a minute that what you are trying to tell me is true," she blustered on, "and everybody in the whole wide world has sinned. What is the solution in that scenario? How can all those people ever be happy?"

"You mention there the whole wide world," Martin continued, in immediate response to her question on whole world happiness. "Listen to this." Then skimming through his Bible he stopped at a page, and started to read, 'For God so loved the world, that he gave his only begotten Son, that whosoever believeth in him should not perish, but have everlasting life'.

"And what does that mean then?" Joanna probed.

Martin proceeded to tell her what that meant, and in the process to inform her of what he believed to be the solution to her predicament.

"Everyone in the world is a sinner. Born in sin. But because God loved the world of sinners he sent his son Jesus, into this world to die on a cross to take away the punishment for their sin," he explained. "And as it says, whoever believes on him will have everlasting life. That means they will have their sin taken away and will consequently be free from the ultimate penalty of that sin."

Joanna stopped him. Held up her hand, like a policewoman at a busy traffic junction. This was all rather too much for her. All at one go.

"Does that mean I cannot do anything to make myself happy?" she countered.

Then without waiting for Martin's reply, she dived into her battery of books, selecting the third book down out of a pile of five, from one of her four stacks of five, causing a slipping, sliding, domino-type collapse to occur all over the slippery table.

After Martin had helped her to restore some sort of order to her very local library, Joanna opened the selected volume, and referred to a passage. It was one she had consulted in her quest for the 'Meaning of Life'.

"It says here that 'happiness is a state of perfection which a man can achieve by his own strength or power,'" she stated almost triumphally. "If I can achieve it by my own strength or power, why would anybody need all that you are talking about?"

"But you cannot achieve happiness by your own strength or power," Martin replied, patiently. "The Bible says it is 'not by might nor by power, but by my spirit, saith the Lord ...'"

And so it went on. All evening.

When Martin was leaving around eleven o'clock, after a session of lively but friendly discourse, Joanna had heard many things, but had been convinced of only one thing. She wanted to hear more of what it was that Martin had to say.

She invited him around for another discussion, the next week. And he came. The next week, and the next, and the next. During those ensuing evenings Joanna gradually identified the two main stumbling-blocks she found with Martin and his calm, and confident message. The first was an integral element of what he taught, and the other was a frustration at what he taught it from ...

The death of Christ was a big conundrum.

After Martin had been speaking about this, what seemed to be a central plank of his platform one day, Joanna burst out, in frustration, "Why have you this whole thing about death? If God is God, and God is all powerful, why could he not just save people and let that be it? Why all this talk about death and blood and stuff?'

As usual, Martin referred her to the Bible. He told her about the need for redemption, and how redemption could be effected through the payment of a price. And the price in the Bible was 'the precious blood of Christ' ...

It was this, as she saw it, blinkered obsession with the Bible and its teachings, that gave rise to Joanna's other intellectual, and spiritual irritation.

Prior to each one of those evening exchanges Joanna had done her homework, reading an ever-widening variety of theories and philosophies from an ever-increasing variety of scholarly writings. And before Martin came she would have them piled up on the table. Her ammunition. An arsenal of it.

When Martin arrived he was invariably only armed with one single weapon. His little highlighted Bible.

One evening her exasperation at her mentor's dependence on the one single book, spilled over too.

"The Bible, The Bible, The Bible ..." she repeated. "Why do you always and only refer to the Bible? I have a whole wall covered with books behind you there, and a dozen or so more on the table in front of you, and still I don't know what's going on! And you are trying to tell me the Bible and what it teaches about salvation is enough!"

"Yes, Joanna, that's true," Martin replied, calmly. "It is enough. I believe the Bible to be the Living Word of God. Listen to this ..." He then leafed through the Bible before him, and read aloud. 'Search the scriptures; for in them ye think ye have eternal life: and they are they which testify of me.'

His reason for reading the Bible even came from the Bible! The fact that Martin never lost his temper, always appeared cool, calm and collected, sometimes maddened Joanna. But mostly it impressed her.

After their fourth session Joanna determined something else. If the Bible was the Living Word Of God, and Martin was so totally dependent on it for all his beliefs, she needed one, too, despite her continuing doubts.

So, after some searching in the bookshops and church shops of Krakow, Joanna eventually found, and bought herself, her first Bible.

When he first saw her with it Martin was moved.

He believed that the Spirit of God had begun to work in Joanna's life.

Joanna believed that she was merely furthering her frustrating quest for fulfilment.

At their next few sessions she began to mark the places that Martin referred to in her newly acquired reference book.

As spring progressed through March, and then marched on through into April, and the buds on the trees in the Planty began slowing opening to herald in a new summer season, Joanna found her own mind, gradually, if even reluctantly, opening itself to the prospect of a new discovery.

Though inwardly she resisted the logic of it, rebelled against the simplicity of it, and tried to find a million reasons to refute it deep, deep, down she had come to admit something she had never dreamt she would do.

She wouldn't dare tell him either. But Martin was right.

He was handling the Living Word of God.

And it was holding the light at the end of her tunnel.

That light was growing brighter, too.

21

TOMORROW WILL BE SPECIAL

It was Good Friday night, 9th April, 1993.

Joanna had been working late in the University of Fine Arts to complete a painting before she set off for her studio apartment, and her Easter vacation. The cobbled streets of Krakow's old quarter through which she walked were becoming crowded with people hurrying along to enjoy a variety of entertainments at the beginning of the holiday weekend. The steady, relentless rain, however, was serving to dampen everyone's spirits and by the time Joanna reached her car where it was parked, well away from the University, she was thoroughly soaked.

After a ten minute drive she arrived back at her own studio, and hung her wet clothes up to dry.

What did the rain, or even a thorough soaking, matter? She was on holiday, and going away for a few days.

As soon as she felt dry and comfortable Joanna began packing. She was packing for tomorrow.

Tomorrow was the day she had been eagerly anticipating for at least the past three weeks.

For tomorrow she would be on vacation.

And tomorrow she had planned to drive the one hundred and twenty miles to the city where her mother lived, and spend the weekend with her.

Tomorrow would be special.

Conducting constant mental checks, Joanna collected together all the items she intended taking with her, on her weekend away. Some of them, like clothes and some smaller incidentals she placed in either one of the two bags on her bedroom floor. The larger items, such as the few paintings she wanted to take to show her mother, her folding easel and a box containing paints, palettes and brushes she left out in the hallway, ready to be picked up in the morning.

It would be a long journey next day, and it would be good to make an early start.

When satisfied that she was as well prepared as she could be for her tomorrow-morning-trip Joanna went to bed. But not to sleep. At once.

Joanna never went to bed, to sleep, at once.

She always tried to read herself to sleep. There was so much she felt she still had to read, so much she still felt she did not know.

And she was still engaged in this endless, restless, hunt for happiness.

Sliding her precious prize, her John Donne poetry book, out from the clutter of books, magazines, empty envelopes and long since letters on her bedside table, she let it fall open at the Holy Sonnets and began to read the page before her.

She had opened at the sonnet with a big V above it. Number five.

It was strange that no matter where she was, or what she read, for the past few months since she had first discussed it with Martin, Joanna did not seem to be able to escape this subject of sin.

And here it came again. Creeping, not leaping, up at her …

'I am a little world made cunningly
Of Elements, and an Angelike spright,
But black sin hath betrayed to endless night
My worlds both parts, and (oh) both parts must die …,'

'Black sin … endless night … both parts must die …,'

It all sounded so bleak, but although Joanna had lived in that black, bleak world for months, Martin had told her that life did not have to be like that for ever and always. There was, he maintained, a solution …

When she had returned her book to its place on her bedside table, Joanna drifted off into sleep, dreaming of tomorrow.

Regardless of the ominous clouds of utter wretchedness which often seemed to obliterate any lightness or brightness from the sky of her life, she hoped that her Easter holiday, away at her mother's, would bring at least a temporary intermission in her misery.

Tomorrow she hoped would be better.

Tomorrow would be special ...

When she opened her eyes that next morning, day light had begun to sneak in through a chink in the curtains, and a gap below, between them and the window.

It was the long-awaited Easter Saturday morning.

The rain of the previous evening had gone and now the sun had risen on a new day. Even before she opened the curtains Joanna's room was bathed in brightness.

But there was more to it than that.

Normally when she opened her eyes in the morning Joanna closed them again instantly. She wanted to block out the prospect of another fourteen hours of mental anguish for as long as possible. Leave waking up to face the world to the last possible moment.

That Saturday morning as soon as she opened her eyes all of a sudden she was wide awake. And stayed that way.

For that morning she was conscious of something unusual.

Joanna had awakened from a nightmare-free night's sleep with God on her mind.

All at once she knew for certain that there was a God. That God was.

And that God was Almighty.

She sat up in bed, slowly, wondering what was happening to her.

Then she became aware of something else. Something both sinister and soothing simultaneously.

God was. God was Almighty. And God was present with her in her room.

It seemed that this invisible presence was directing her to reflect of all the weeks and weeks of meditations with Martin.

She was not permitted to deliberate upon those discussions in a random, haphazard, take-it-or-leave it fashion, however. No. This was different. Either weird or wonderful. Or both.

All the topics she and Martin had talked about at different times, and as far as she was concerned, with different levels of conviction, formed themselves up in her mind, in an orderly line waiting to pop forward, in a particular pattern.

'I am a sinner ... God loves me ... Jesus died on the cross for my sins to clear me ... and to cleanse me ... He loved me so much ... should I not love Him too? ...'

Joanna reached out to her bedside table again. This time it was not for her poetry book, but for her recently acquired Bible. She would read one of the verses she had marked in it. One of the verses Martin had often mentioned.

Flicking through it, she found one.

It was John chapter five and the twenty-fourth verse.

She read, slowly, carefully ...

'Verily, verily, I say unto you, He that heareth my word, and believeth on him that sent me, hath everlasting life, and shall not come into condemnation; but is passed from death unto life.'

Closing the Bible gently Joanna replaced it on the table. She was a tiny bit disappointed. She had hoped for some sudden revelation but had not been given it. All that about condemnation and everlasting life was a bit beyond her yet.

Although unable to understand the verse Joanna had no doubt about what she understood in her heart.

She believed in God. This was in itself a giant step forward for someone who up until that point had even doubted the existence of God.

She believed that Jesus died on the cross for the sin of the world. And for her sin, too.

That also represented a massive leap forward.

Her most significant acknowledgment of all, though, was the recognition of the desire to have God and Jesus as part of her entire life from that moment onward.

Sitting up straight in the bed she whispered, softly, simply and sincerely, "Lord, forgive me!"

Suddenly Joanna's heart began to beat really fast.

She had no idea what was happening to her, but she was sure of two things. One was, that whatever it was, it was of prime importance, and the other was that she needed help.

She rose, washed, dressed and with her heart still aflutter, and without even considering having anything to eat, she went out to her telephone, looked through the little battered book beside it, and then dialled 3-3-9-7-6-3. To Martin. It was only when she tried to spin the dial that she realised her fingers were shaking uncontrollably!

Although Joanna didn't realise what it was that was happening, Martin did, and he told her that he would be with her within fifteen minutes. And he was, with his Bible, having walked all the way and prayed all the way!

When she had recounted to him her experiences of that morning to date, and it was still only nine-thirty, Martin said that he would pray, and after he had prayed then she could pray, and talk to God.

Then Martin began to pray, and to pray specifically for her. This was the first time Joanna had ever heard anyone address God on her behalf, and for the first few minutes she found it strange. Then it became warm, and reassuring. Here was somebody who was obviously in touch with God, preparing the way for her to make that vital link, also.

When he had finished Martin lifted his head, looked across the room and across the table, across which he had patiently presented Joanna with the truths of the Bible, and invited simply, "Now you pray, Joanna."

Although not nearly as long as Martin's, or not couched in such spiritual language, Joanna's prayer, when she bowed her head and prayed aloud, was no less sincere.

"God, I am a sinner," she said simply. "I know Jesus died for me. Please come into my heart and life and change me for ever."

When her short prayer was finished she opened her eyes and looked over at Martin.

He was looking back, his face beaming.

"Now that you have trusted in Christ you are saved, Joanna," be told her. "You are a child of God. Now you can pray to Him, and read the Bible." Then he added, with a twinkle in his eye, "The Living Word of God.'"

Joanna was now happier than she could ever remember having been for some time. If she had ever been so happy.

She felt for the first time in her whole life that the burden of blackness was beginning to lift from around her. It was burning off like the mist that used to hang over the tops of the Tatras until the sun came out.

Martin advised her about a number of aspects of 'the Christian life' as he called it, but on his way out, about half an -hour later, he repeated one point.

"Remember what I told you, Joanna. Look out for the devil. Don't be surprised if he tries to make you doubt this experience, or block you or weaken you in anyone of dozens of different ways."

With that the door closed behind him. He was gone. Joanna was alone.

For the first time in her entire life, however, she was acutely aware that she was not alone. God was with her, in her studio and in her life.

Now, though, it was time to make final preparations for the trip for which she was already partially prepared. And to which she had so much been looking forward …

As she put the finishing touches to her packing, Joanna began to feel unwell. She could not understand how that, within the space of an hour since Martin left, she had begun to feel sick. Waves of nausea swept over her.

Then when she went into the bathroom, a further shock was in store.

Just as she walked in through the door she saw herself in a mirror.

Her face was absolutely covered in red blotches! A further frantic examination revealed that they were on her arms, her legs, her body. She had a rash all over her!

Although she had begun to feel physically under the weather, Joanna had an unusual peace in her heart, and a strong desire in her mind to fulfil the expectation of that weekend. She would drive to her mother's even it did take longer than usual, and she could rest for as long as she liked when she got there.

That was the plan.

Then there occurred complication number two.

Having placed all her baggage outside, Joanna went to lock her front door before leaving, and despite all her efforts she could not turn the key in the lock!

It was broken. No matter how hard she tried she could not lock her front door!

Another dilemma!

She could not leave her studio with almost a year's paintings in it, until she was sure it was firmly secured.

In desperation she phoned her dad, and in less than an hour he was over with her.

Michael Maciantowicz took one look at his daughter and exclaimed, "What is wrong with you, Joanna?"

"I don't know," came the reply from the now much weaker Joanna. "I don't feel all that well!"

"You don't look all that well either!" came the concerned father's immediate retort. "I will fix the lock on this door and then you can come over to our flat and go to bed. We will look after you, until you are feeling a bit better."

"But …but …" Joanna began to protest. "I was planning to go to see mother today."

"You are certainly not fit to be driving that far in that state!" her father told her emphatically.

"I suppose you are right," his now feeling-even-more-rotten daughter was forced to concede.

Before lunch time on that long-awaited Saturday Joanna's plans for the day had been turned upside down.

When she arrived back at her father's flat, Elizabeth, who was a nurse, saw the pathetic figure as she came struggling in and said, "You can have my bed, Joanna. You look like a typical case of German measles to me."

In the middle of the afternoon Joanna lay tucked up in a freshly changed bed. The bedroom faced south and the whole room was full of warmth and sunlight.

Despite feeling physically sick, and despite the blotches all over her body, Joanna felt at peace, for the first time in her life.

As she lay there she reflected on the events of the previous eight or ten hours.

She had expected to be well on her way by now, off on her much-anticipated Easter vacation and instead here she was lying ill, but at ease, in bed.

That was a turn of events she could never have possibly imagined, even in her wildest dreams.

But something even much more significant and spectacular than that had happened, too.

That morning she had been awakened by a consciousness of the reality and presence of God. Now she had placed a simple faith in Christ and was basking in the light of His love.

It seemed, as she lay in that sunlit room, that not only had she discovered the light at the end of her tunnel of darkness, but that the tunnel of darkness itself had totally disappeared. Everything was light and bright around her.

In the hours that followed many images floated through her artistic mind. In one of those she compared herself to a restless, turbulent, bubbling stream, broken into seething foam by jagged rocks. For twenty-four years she had been like that. Now though, her stream had reached the tranquil sea, and had been swallowed up in the indescribable peace that comes with being at one with an all loving, ever-caring God.

The previous night Joanna had gone to sleep in the firm conviction that tomorrow would be different.

And she had been right in that prediction.

'Tomorrow' had cancelled out all her yesterdays.

'Tomorrow' had been special.

22

THE BLOCK AND THE BRIDGE

It was three weeks before Joanna was well enough to return to University, and when she did Martin was anxiously awaiting news of her. He had heard that she had been ill, but on learning that her complaint was nothing more serious than German measles, he was not worried about her physical condition. Her spiritual condition concerned him more.

How was she coping in her newly-found faith? Martin need not have worried.

When he first met Joanna on return to University he was delighted to discover that she was still so happy. All the gloom had gone. The doubt and despair had disappeared. The endless questions had been replaced by a calm assurance.

Joanna was a different person altogether.

She seemed so confident. So relaxed. So at peace. Recognising that she would need much encouragement to help her grow as a Christian, Martin recommended that she try visiting Krakow Baptist Church on a Sunday morning.

Joanna was so grateful to Martin for his earlier patient counsel that she was quite willing to respond to his suggestion and on the next Sunday morning made her way to the Baptist Church.

And what a revelation that proved to be for the young Christian! For nearly a month now Joanna had been basking in the heat and light of the love of God.

She had been avidly reading the Living Word of God.

She had begun to derive great consolation from praying to an all-caring, all-controlling God.

She had, however, been doing all that on her own.

When she arrived at the Baptist Church that first Sunday morning and was warmly welcomed, it came as a tremendous thrill to Joanna to discover that Martin and she were not the only two Christians in Krakow!

In that church that morning there were about one hundred people, men, women and children. They all appeared to have their own Bibles with them and all those she spoke to seemed to have known for years what she had just discovered. Peace and joy and satisfaction.

She found it moving when the children sang about it,

> 'I've got joy, joy, joy, joy,
> Down in my heart,
> Down in my heart ...'

Then they went on to sing another verse which said,

> 'I've got the peace that passes understanding,
> Down in my heart,
> Down in my heart ...'

That was how she felt. Precisely. And here she was in a church, almost full of people who seemed to feel exactly the same.

Fantastic!

'I will be back here,' Joanna promised herself, half-way through the service. 'This is great.'

When the meetings for the week were announced later, Joanna thought that it would be good to go along to something called 'the late prayer meeting' on the Friday evening at ten o'clock. Up until now she had been praying to God on her own. It would surely be good to pray along with others. In a 'prayer meeting'. It sounded like a good way to end the week.

Next Friday though, things did not work out just as Joanna had planned.

Early in the evening a number of her friends from University had come around to her studio to discuss their work, their examinations at the end of the year, and their plans for the summer.

The exchanges were lively, the deliberations on each other's paintings often technical and protracted, and what worried Joanna was that nobody seemed to be in the slightest hurry to go home. Or indeed go anywhere. They looked as though they would still be there at midnight!

The new Christian was determined though.

She wanted to go to the prayer meeting in the Baptist church. She had her heart set on it.

At nine-thirty Joanna announced, with a laugh, "I am not putting anybody out but I have an important meeting to attend at ten o'clock on the other side of town!"

"O.K. Joanna, we can take a hint!" one of her guests replied, laughing herself. "We will go now!"

As they were filtering out of her studio one of the young men who had never been there before asked, "Joanna, how do I get home from here?"

"That's not difficult," the leaving-also hostess replied. "I am coming now, too. You drive your car down to the crossroads and I will follow you in mine. Then I will jump out and point you in the right direction."

Good idea. All sounded so simple.

However, when they reached the crossroads, and Joanna jumped out of her car to give the other driver the necessary directions, something happened. How it happened she didn't know, but it happened.

The driver's door of her car was locked when she went back to it!

There was no way she could open it.

Frantically she tried the other door of her two-door red Metro. It was also locked. She had only opened the driver's door when she had come to the car.

Her friend in the car in front saw her dilemma, parked his own car, and came back.

Together they tried everything.

The boot was locked. No way in there.

There was no hope of anything through the windows, either. They were all tightly closed.

Joanna felt so frustrated. The complete mystery and embarrassing stupidity of the situation were soon overtaken in her mind by the potential dangers.

The engine was still running, and since she had only recently started the car, the choke was on. Billows of white choking smoke poured from the exhaust.

The other man, who felt somehow responsible for Joanna's predicament, said he had an iron bar in the car. In panic they tried to prise open the driver's door but to no avail. They merely succeeded in damaging it.

Now steam had begun to rise from below the bonnet also. The engine was overheating.

How long would it be until the car went on fire?

By now a crowd had gathered around and one man who seemed to know about cars said he thought that if he had a screwdriver he could take out a back window. Someone soon offered to supply him with whatever tools he needed, and within ten anxious minutes he had the back window out, a door opened, and the engine switched off.

The car, though, could not now be driven.

The engine would have to be left to cool down and more water added to the radiator. And that would be the simplest solution.

What if the hanging, clinging, acrid smell of burning rubber was the symptom of some more serious problem?

The friend to whom Joanna had given the directions, and who had remained with her throughout the smoking-steaming car dilemma, brought her back to her studio.

Just after she had thrown herself down in a chair in deep disappointment she looked at the clock. It was after midnight.

The prayer meeting would be over. And everybody would be back home. In bed, probably, the most of them.

Then she remembered Martin's admonition of her salvation Saturday morning. 'The devil will try to block you,' was what he had warned.

That strange car-locking over-heating window-breaking situation had been one of Satan's blocks.

'I can see now what Martin meant,' she concluded. 'He has succeeded tonight,' she conceded.

'But he won't succeed the next time!' she determined.

Next morning Joanna was reading her Bible. She had heard someone in the Baptist Church refer to 'the twenty-third Psalm' and on a number of occasions in that week she had read it. And every time she read it she seemed to see something different in it.

That morning it was a phrase in verse five that struck her as significant.

'Thou preparest a table before me in the presence of mine enemies ...' she read. 'The presence of mine enemies ...' Joanna was beginning to prove practically what Martin had told her. Christians do have enemies. The devil would try to block her.

The wonderful part about it, though, was that no matter what enemies she had, or how strong they were, God had promised to prepare a table of ample provision, for her, in their presence.

Her God was peace, and power, and provision, all personified. And Joanna continued to rejoice in her position as one of His children by faith. She was almost daily thrilled by some new discovery from the Bible. Something which often had her exclaiming in praise, "Thank you. Thank you, Lord!"

She had also come to love the services in the Baptist Church, but unfortunately since she was very often out of Krakow at the weekends, either visiting friends or family, or on painting trips from University, she could not attend every week.

However, one Sunday in late May, when she was free to be there, Joanna had a pleasant surprise.

For there, in the morning service in the Baptist Church she noticed one of her art teachers from the University sitting up in front of her, with his wife and children. She had always liked this man, who was both a gifted artist and a respected teacher. Now Joanna knew what it was that was different about him.

This teacher was a Christian.

After the service Joanna spoke to him and told him how she come to be there. Of her struggle in the search for truth and light and peace, about her commitment to Christ, about Martin's suggestion that she attend the Baptist Church...

What pleased her most was the fact that her teacher seemed as delighted to hear what she had to say, as she was delighted to tell him.

On her way home in the car that morning Joanna felt even more at peace. The presence at the Church of that lecturer who was so admired by his students had inspired her.

It was, she thought, an important link. He was her bridge between Art school and God's school.

Now she felt even more fulfilled. For now she was not only at peace in herself and with God, but she had found a place where she could worship God amongst others who loved Him too.

It was marvellous.

So satisfying.

23

THAT ONE'S MINE!

It was almost the end of the academic year.

June 1993.

The University of Fine Arts in Krakow was buzzing with life. Students were busy preparing their work for examination and exhibition, both in the University and beyond.

Joanna was hurrying up the broad stone stairs to an upper storey. She had just passed the sculptures on the first landing and had begun to skip up the second flight, two steps at a time, when she was conscious of another woman coming down.

This lady looked lost.

She held out the hand holding the notebook to try and slow down the rapidly-approaching, flying, flapping student, all beads and bandanna.

"Excuse me," she began, apologetically, "you seem to be in a hurry, but I wonder if you could help me?"

Joanna drew herself up to a breathless halt.

"Yes, certainly," she panted. "What can I do for you?"

The visitor was a tall, slim woman with long dark hair which fell down loosely on to the shoulders of a stylish gabardine raincoat which swished around her as she walked. She had dark piercing eyes.

There was something, if not beautiful, certainly attractive, in a stately sort of sense, about this stranger. She oozed elegance.

The held out hand held a notebook, and the other a leather briefcase with shiny buckles. This young lady had the air of a business woman who meant business.

"My name is Andrea. I represent a company from Dresden in Germany and we are hoping to sponsor two artists for the next academic year, starting in September," the visitor began to explain hastily, obviously glad to have found someone who looked as though she could help her, if she could only get her breath back. "Who should I contact, or where could I go to see some art work? It is particularly painting we are interested in."

An idea sprang into Joanna's mind at once but she needed one more item of information to render it feasible.

"A lot depends on how long you have to spend," Joanna replied, paving the way to procuring the facts she required.

"I am planning to stay in Krakow overnight so I will have the remainder of today and most of tomorrow," the visitor volunteered.

That was all Joanna needed to know.

"In that case then I think the best thing to do would be for you to come to our 'view'," she advised. "We are preparing for an exhibition in Maastricht and over the next two days all the people in our painting classes have been invited to display any work they wished to have considered for exhibition."

"That sounds good to me," the aspiring sponsor replied, "Will there be much work there?"

"Yes there will. You will see a complete range of art work there," Joanna "There will be lots and lots of students, and lots and lots of drawings and paintings. Some folks bring albums of photos of their work. Some bring one or two of their best paintings. Some bring their whole portfolio. It will take you all the time you have to see all the stuff!"

That was exactly what Andrea, as she had introduced herself, wanted. It would give her the chance to observe the work of a wide range of students in her own time. And without any pressure.

So Andrea did as Joanna had suggested.

She hovered around, notebook at the ready, as students by the score came and went. Joanna had been right. Within the space of two half-days, an afternoon and the following morning, she had seen single paintings, photos of paintings, portfolios of paintings. There were hundreds of them, all shapes and sizes, ranging from the utterly traditional to the ultra-modem.

All the students knew that to have paintings selected for the Maastricht exhibition would give them a unique opportunity to present their work in the world's shop window. So they brought their best to the 'view'.

After lunch time on the second day Andrea found Joanna for a second time.

Not this time because she had bumped into her, but because she had gone looking for her.

"I hope you do not mind me asking, Joanna," she said, "but I need your help again."

Joanna had watched the dark-haired sponsor moving amongst the work on display a few times and realised that there was more to her than her imposing appearance. She had an eye for art. It should be no hardship to help her.

"Again it will be a pleasure to do what I can," Joanna volunteered.

Andrea was all business. She came straight to the point. Didn't waffle about.

"I have chosen two paintings from all that I have seen," she said. "I wonder if you know the artists and if you do could you tell me how to contact them?"

"Show me where they are and I will do my best," Joanna told her, secretly curious to discover who was going to be offered the sponsorship.

The first painting Andrea pointed out was of birds, obviously sea-birds, white birds with black-wing tips skimming over rolling waves on a rocky shore. A dark cloud in the background gave the impression of an impending storm.

When that painting had first appeared on the view Joanna had liked it. There was something simply dramatic and compelling about it. She knew too who had painted it.

"That one's Bertha's," she said. "I know Bertha. I can put you in contact with her O.K."

Then swinging around from Bertha's birds, the discerning art sponsor walked across to the other side of the hall in resolute manner.

She seemed to know what she wanted. And she seemed to know where it was.

Joanna followed her, wondering, wondering …

Stopping in front of a large painting on the opposite wall of the hall Andrea said simply, "That's the other one."

It was a striking picture. Striking for the strength of its simplicity. The focal point of the painting was a central figure, a girl, dressed all in white. She was kneeling down surrounded by rays of light streaming in from the top left hand comer. This light shining on the visible side of her face gave it a warm, heavenly glow.

All around the girl was a background of a strong red colour. And that was all there was to it.

The girl in white. The pervading light. The eye-catching red. Three elements. That was all.

The painting was so compelling, however, that Andrea had been arrested by it. Many had commented on it during the two days of the 'view', and it had already been earmarked for Maastricht.

Joanna could feel herself blushing slightly. "That one's mine," she whispered softly.

It felt like a fix. But it wasn't.

Andrea could not possibly have had any idea of the painter of the girl bathed in heavenly light. And very few could have had any idea of the mental and spiritual experiences which had inspired it.

What Joanna had actually done was 'give her testimony' as she had heard some of the kind Baptist people call it, on canvas, with paint and brushes.

In July, Joanna and Bertha set off for Dresden where they met the executives from the manufacturing company GEERS, and a sponsorship deal was arranged. Under the terms of the agreement the company were to sponsor the two girls for their final year at University and they in turn were to submit twenty paintings each for an exhibition which the company would help arrange.

Nor was that all. Late in August the sponsors, who manufactured audio aids came to Krakow to mount a sales drive in a shop selling hearing aids and other audio equipment. Joanna had been invited to display a few of her paintings at the shop for the duration of the company's involvement.

One day in the shop a lady was seeking out the "artist who did these lovely paintings'.

When Joanna presented herself the lady introduced herself.

"I am from the Deaf and Dumb Institute here in Krakow," she said. "We have been looking out for some one for quite a while to teach painting, just for a few hours per week. Would you consider doing something like that? We would pay teacher's hourly rates."

Joanna was delighted with this offer, too. And accepted it. Walking back to her car, from the shop that day, Joanna was forced to reflect upon what was happening in her life.

She had been awarded art sponsorship for a year. She had been offered a part-time job teaching art. And she hadn't applied for anything.

Joanna was now living and walking in the light that she had so much craved, and had painted in her picture.

God had taken the helm of her life.

And the voyage with Him only just begun!

24

DAYBREAK

The summer of 1993 was one long dawn for Joanna.

Almost every day she read from her Bible, learnt at the Baptist Church or experienced in her life something new, something different, something exciting to the extent of being stunning, about her position and privileges as a Christian.

God does not introduce His daylight suddenly upon the earth. Daybreak comes gradually. First a grey light in the sky, then the sun rising over the rim of the horizon. It is many hours later before the full heat and light of midday can be enjoyed.

For Joanna the experience of salvation was like that. It was like wakening up in the morning just as the shades of night are being overtaken and overcome by the light and bright of approaching day.

The dawning of the daylight of peace upon her soul, the first light to cross her horizon of blackness, took place on Easter Saturday. It was only gradually after that, however, that she began to appreciate all the riches of peace and joy which were set to flow from that experience.

At first all was shadowy and silhouetted. Everything was present but not easily discernible. As light increased so she began to identify shapes, but then she saw sizes, too. Gradually delicate shades of colour appeared ... Day was progressing.

Like the Buddhist 'master's' cord, this increasing awareness of Joanna's had a variety of coloured strands woven into it, each one different to the other, and yet in a strange way that appealed immediately to a sensitive artist, each one complementary to the other.

The first of these came with an avid desire to read her Bible. It was only now that she could understand why Martin had been so fond of his. In her eager frequent reading she daily discovered new thoughts and truths which helped her sketch out in her mind an outline of God, the world and herself. And the interrelation of each to the other.

Every reading added a new shade of colour, a different perspective, a developing foreground, or a broad and beautiful backdrop.

One morning in her reading she discovered Psalm twenty-seven. She read it over and over many times and then spent the remainder of the day quoting to herself the first verse ...' The Lord is my light and my salvation; whom shall I fear? the Lord is the strength of my life; of whom shall I be afraid?'

It was so thrilling! 'The Lord is my light ...'

For years Joanna had been searching for the light at the end of her tunnel of darkness, and now she had found that light. What was more she could express the most important and the most profound discovery of her entire lifetime in five simple words!

'The Lord is my light ...'!

As she continued to read her Bible and attend church Joanna was increasingly arrested by the greatness and power and might of her God, her Lord, her Light and her Peace. The contrast between the comfort and consolation of 'God is love,' and the awesome concept of 'Holy, holy, holy, is the Lord of hosts: the whole earth is full of his glory,' enthralled her.

It was not only in her scripture reading and church attendance that the light and warmth of the developing day in her discovery of God occurred, however. There were certain occasions when suddenly, surprisingly, she would stumble upon something that would immediately direct her mind back to God and the joy she was finding in discovering Him. Every such revelation gave her the thrill of having unwrapped an unexpected Christmas gift to discover yet another Christian jewel.

She had an experience like that one afternoon, when she was sitting in her studio idly leafing through a book on the history of Art. As a page fell open Joanna's attention was gripped by the word 'God'. Holding the book open at that place she began to read. What she had happened upon was a quotation by Fra Angelico, an early fifteenth century Italian painter. It said,

'God is a living splendour, woven of love, wisdom and power.

'Welcome it, greet it, and touch the angel's hand that brings it.

'Take courage then to claim it.

'Take courage in the knowledge that we are pilgrims wending through an unknown country on our way home.'

'God is a living splendour'. What a description!

One of the most profound mysteries that this new Christian had to cope with on her voyage into the sunlight of God's love was the fact that this mighty God was ever interested in her. And that feeling was intensified when she came to the full realisation of what she was in herself, and in God's sight, before He intervened in her life.

Martin had talked to her about sin, and showed her from the Bible that 'all have sinned and come short of the glory of God'.

On two occasions she felt almost overcome with emotion and thankfulness when this fact burst upon her. These experiences hit her, not with the slow enlightenment of daybreak but with the sudden illumination afforded by the switching on of an electric light in a darkened room. When once sampled, however, these further manifestations help contribute to the daybreak unfolding in her soul.

The first came on a Sunday morning service in the Baptist Church in Krakow. Joanna had begun to make other friends there in addition to her University teacher and his wife, and attended every Sunday she was at home. And there she learnt so many new things about her new faith.

That Sunday morning a hymn was sung and Joanna thought both the words and tune of it were beautiful. It summed her up so well. As the congregation sang it lustily she could barely sing for revelling in the words. They were singing:-

'Amazing grace! How sweet the sound
That saved a wretch like me.
I once was lost, but now am found,
Was blind, but now I see.

'Twas grace that taught my heart to fear,
And grace my fears relieved.
How precious did that grace appear
The hour I first believed ...'

That hymn introduced another word into her increasing spiritual vocabulary, and another concept into her increasing spiritual understanding. Grace. The unlimited favour of God. No wonder the person who wrote that hymn could say it was 'amazing', Joanna mused. At that time she knew nothing of John Newton and his heartfelt appreciation of God's grace. All she knew was that it took 'amazing grace' to 'save a wretch' like her.

> 'How precious did that grace appear
> The hour I first believed ...'

'How precious', indeed!

Joanna was daily uncovering more precious facets to this sparkling gem of grace.

With the zest with which Joanna threw herself into Bible study it was only to be expected that the other time when she was led to recognise in a very real way what God had done for her was when she was reading 'The Living Word of God', as Martin often called it. Her poetic bent found her turning, as though attracted by some mighty magnet, to the Psalms, time and time again.

And it was when reading the one hundred and sixteenth Psalm that she discovered her whole experience of God, and what he had done for her succinctly summarised in three pithy phrases.

'Thou hast delivered my soul from death, mine eyes from tears, and my feet from falling,' was what it said.

'That's my life', Joanna thought, 'and how true the description is, on each and every count'.

The promised presence of God in her life was another shaft of sunlight in the developing radiance of Joanna's spiritual day.

It excited her, and often sent a chill down her spine to realise that God was now present with her all the time, too. The assurance of Scripture verses which she heard such as, 'Lo, I am with you alway', and 'I will never leave thee, nor forsake thee' she found almost unbelievable. It was fantastic to think that God was ever present in her life and He had pledged to be there, 'alway'.

The greatest privilege of all Joanna discovered, however, in her newly found faith in Christ was linked to this enjoyment of an ever present, ever loving, ever caring God and Saviour.

This was the privilege of prayer.

She did not now have to pray into a vacuum She did not have to begin her prayers as she had once done, 'God, IF You are really there …' For now Joanna knew that God was really there, and that He was ready to hear and to answer her prayer. Wherever or whenever she prayed it. She was a child of God coming to her Heavenly Father.

It was all so thrilling!

Daybreak had happened.

The spiritual sun was shining in all its splendour.

And yet Joanna had still lots to learn about the light which had dispelled the darkness at the end of her tunnel.

The light which had become the illumination of her life.

25

SHOOTING STARS

It was during that summer of spiritual daybreak also, that Joanna went off, with a number of her friends, to spend a few days in a summer hut, deep in the heart of the Polish countryside, many miles from Krakow.

Everyone was so relaxed. The weather was good and this in turn made everybody feel good. It gave them a lift. In addition to the pleasant summer heat, a sense of endless inner satisfaction and light, life and peace in her soul, allowed Joanna, particularly, to feel great.

One of the nights on that holiday was so bright and so balmy that no-one wanted to return to their bunks. Millions of stars stabbed the blackness of the sky with pinpricks of light whose cumulative effect was to illuminate the surrounding with a blue-light light-blue glow.

The whole group sat around the campfire they had lit, for hours, chatting, laughing, discussing everything. Midnight passed. Friday had given way to Saturday, but still they stayed out. Some of the group sat up gazing pensively into the fire. Others lay around reclining, heads propped up on elbows, while the light from the flames painted firelight fantasies on their faces.

Joanna was one of those who were sitting forward, staring fixedly into the fire. Although she was conscious of the conversation going on around her, and adding her own comment from time to time, her immediate preoccupation was with the spluttering spurting flames.

What pictures she saw in that fire!

There were beautiful birds with wide wings flying off into the sunset. There were sharp-pointed, powerful rockets preparing to pierce the unknown, followed by fingers of fire.

There were children on a sandy beach at sunrise, their running playful figures engulfed in an early morning golden glow ...

Then suddenly the tranquillity of the countryside fireside was cracked open by one of the group, a girl, shouting, "Oh look!"

All heads turned towards her, and then all eyes followed her pointing hand up into the star-studded sky.

There could be no doubt about what had so attracted this girl. And why she had been so anxious for all her friends to 'Oh look!' at what she had seen.

There, zooming across the brilliant night sky was a huge shooting star, a trail of silver light flowing out behind it.

Instinctively, on seeing that shooting star Joanna offered up to the Creator of the heaven and the earth, the One whose light had lit up her life, and whose sky that night was ablaze with stars, a simple prayer.

It was a prayer that was a wish.

It was the prayer of a young Christian. And the wish of a young woman.

"God, if there is somewhere out there a man for me, please will You bring him to me," she breathed inwardly, but ardently.

Someone poked the fire.

Showers of spitting sparks shot up into the summer night. They looked like fireflies as they rose up, up, up and away.

When she saw the life and light in those sparks Joanna wondered if they were a sign of something? Was there still more life and light ahead for her? A life and a light of a different kind?

Twenty minutes later, long before everyone had finished deliberating and speculating on the last one, there was another shooting star, tracing a track across the sky.

Nobody needed to shout to anybody now for most people were staring compulsively up to the sky anyway, since it was the focal point of all their astronomical observations.

Again Joanna began, "Oh God if You please ..." She could barely finish her prayer-wish the second time. She felt so self-conscious and silly saying it somehow, but the desire, the sentiment, was still very much in her heart.

Very few of that group even retired to the hut that night until day began to break, for all throughout the night there had been so many stars shooting, and falling across the sky.

It was like a heavenly fireworks display.

And every single time Joanna saw one of them, whilst all her companions were making all sorts of comments, she was reiterating her heart's desire.

It was never expressed with the same passion as the initial outburst but it was nonetheless every bit as passionate. By the time the night of the shooting stars was over Joanna's prayer had become abbreviated to 'Please, God,' or 'Oh God'. Towards morning it had become truncated completely to the plain recognition of his presence and power in the single word, 'God'.

There could be no doubt that the God whom she had come to love, and to speak to in prayer dozens of times a day, would know what she meant.

After the holiday, back in Krakow, Joanna and some of the friends who had been with her by the fire by the hut on the night of the Heavenly Power and Design Exhibition, met some other of their friends who had not been with them on that memorable night.

Those who had remained at home in the city were all full of what they had seen of the shooting stars and what everyone on radio and TV had been saying about the astronomical reasons for, and significance of, it all.

The other two girls and the one young man who just happened to be with Joanna both in the country and at that on-the-pavement review, said enthusiastically, and with that now tell us something we don't know attitude, "Yes, we know. We saw it! We were there! We sat up all night watching it! It was fantastic!"

And as they talked, Joanna stood in silence. She was whispering, to herself, "And I prayed.

And wished.

And prayed.

And wished ..."

26

WHITE LADY

It had rained heavily in the early afternoon of Friday, 10th September, 1993 and the buildings around Krakow's popular Market Square were reflected in a vast flat looking-glass of lying water. The Old Town Hall tower, St. Mary's Church with its two towers, one slightly taller than the other, and the Cloth Hall with its multiple symmetrical arches and ornate architecture were all so perfectly mirrored in the mini-lake that it appeared as though the entire square was completely covered in architectural grandeur.

It seemed slightly incongruous, almost sacrilegious, when the taking-it-easy tourists or the busy locals either wandered slowly or walked briskly across the imposing square. In either case they spoiled the picture by either introducing unwanted figures to it or sending unwanted ripples across it.

As had now become increasingly common for her, Joanna felt an eagerness, a particular zest for life that day. She had painted all morning in her studio and had been satisfied with her work.

Travelling in to the city centre that afternoon after the rain she was overwhelmed with a strange sense of significance. A premonition of importance. Something momentous was about to happen somewhere, somehow, before the end of that day. She just knew.

It promised to be a profitable day.

Joanna met up with her friends at the pre-arranged time and at the pre-arranged place, one of the many colourful street cafes around Rynek Glowny. The cafe which was a favourite haunt of her group was in the comer of the square close to the clock tower. The food was good and reasonable in that particular one and you could see more of the square from there!

As the group of friends sat drinking coffee a slight wind arose and sent natural ripples chasing across the wet square. The gentle wind and the teeny-weeny waves reminded Joanna of the sea, and ships. For a moment she thought that all the water around looked as though it was on the just washed down deck of a ship. And she was on the ship, sailing away, and away, to the north ...

It seemed that another of the group was in sailing away mood too, or perhaps the memory of a successful holiday that year had made him think of his next trip-to-wherever, for he said, "Let's all go away somewhere."

"O.K!" Another girl was willing to take up the challenge. "Where should we go?"

Various places were mentioned and their merits discussed then someone suggested, "How about Ireland?"

"My brother Thomas has been there," Joanna volunteered. "He has been to Ireland."

"Well tell us what it is like then," someone else urged, since Joanna had claimed an Irish contact.

"I'm not awful sure what it is like but I know this, it is very far away, across a lot of seas," she replied. Then, having proved that she was an artist and not a geographer she further went on to prove that she was not a historian either.

"Is Ireland not where those Vikings come from?" she asked the others. "You know the people I mean. The fierce-looking warriors with the big helmets with the horns!"

Nobody was quite sure about that one. Somebody said, "No, I don't think so. Were they not from Norway or Sweden or somewhere like that?"

It was left. Nobody really knew. And nobody really cared. Ireland, or Norway, or Sweden, all seemed a million miles away from one of the largest and most attractive market squares in Europe.

And Joanna needed another drink. All that sailing over imaginary seas and contemplating faraway places was thirsty work.

She rose from the table, leaned in below the red and white sun umbrella to inform her friends at the second table, "I'm going for another drink." She could have called a waitress and asked her to bring her one, but that would take time. Experience had taught her that it was much quicker to go up to the counter inside and order it yourself.

There were two entrances to that cafe. There was the traditional entrance, the door, and there was also a mediaeval arched window which opened outwards and many of the younger customers used it as an additional entrance or exit.

Joanna chose to use the window. Having stepped over the two foot high sill she stopped and leaned against the wooden window frame. Her attention had been drawn to a group of lively tourists who were laughing and passing a floppy sunhat from head to head.

It was like pass the parcel with a hat. Joanna became fascinated by the frolics of these foreigners. What was going to happen to the hat? Who owned it? Where would it end up?

As she continued to follow the fortunes of the unfortunate hat Joanna became conscious that one member of the group had lost interest in the hat. It was passing him by. His eyes were on her. Not the hat.

Hastily Joanna turned and moved across to the counter to order her drink.

There was no escaping the eyes, however. Those big brown eyes were following her every move.

Who was this chap in the red and white striped shirt?

The answer to her question, although she was not to know it immediately, was that he was someone who thought he had seen an angel just lately arrived on earth.

He had been involved in the my hat your hat round the table merriment when he had glanced towards the window to see what the weather was like, and there standing framed in the window was a lady in white. White blouse, white trousers, white shoes. The only two contrasting items in the dress of the white lady were the beads and the bandanna. The three strings of beads around her neck were of different lengths and every conceivable colour, but the bandanna was red. Long and flowing and bright, bright red.

The young man in the red and white striped shirt just could not take his eyes off the young woman in the white blouse and the red bandanna. It was impossible.

His gaze was firmly fixed on her. Nobody, or nothing else mattered.

There was something so appealing, and so appealingly pure, about this person.

For the entire time she stood at that counter waiting to be served, Joanna could feel the big brown eyes boring into her back.

Who was this person who was staring at her? Almost through her?

She was soon to know.

Stepping forward to go out the window again she found that her way had been blocked. By the man with the brown eyes and the striped shirt.

He was about to take a chance. He felt he had to. Never in his whole life had he seen a girl like this and he wasn't going to miss the opportunity to at least make her acquaintance. But could she speak his language?

Here he was in southern Poland. And the girl was Polish. At least he assumed that for he had heard her gibbering away to the woman behind the counter and he hadn't understood a word of what she had been saying. Not one single word.

"Excuse me, you probably don't speak English, but I wonder if maybe you do speak English," he said, embarrassed at the crude clumsiness of the approach when he had finished. But at least the ice was broken.

That was of course providing she understood what he was talking about!

Joanna held her strawberry milkshake out in front of her, smiled across at this friendly foreigner and said calmly, "Yes, I do speak English."

Truth to tell she had taken an instant liking to the lad.

Seeing that he was in a state of suspended shock at her fluent response in his language, she continued to set him at ease by asking, "And where are you from?"

"I'm from Northern Ireland," the young man replied, regaining his composure. His heart was still thumping to get out of his chest, though.

"Northern Ireland!" Joanna exclaimed with a laugh. "That's funny. We were just talking about Ireland out there at the table ten minutes ago. Some of us were thinking about going there for our holidays next year!"

"You would probably like that," the young man responded. Then satisfied that this lovely girl could at least understand him he went on to enquire, "If you don't mind me asking, what's your name?"

"I'm Joanna," the girl replied simply. "And yours?"

"My name is Colin," the chap with the red striped T-shirt and flushed red face went on.

"Are you here on holiday?" Joanna asked.

"Yes," Colin informed her, "I am travelling around Europe with my two friends over there, Ian and Gary." With that he nodded across at his 'two friends over there, Ian and Gary,' who had by that time also abandoned the my hat your head game around the table and were engrossed in the boy meets girl drama being acted out in the middle of the floor.

Ignoring their muttering and whisperings Colin went on to pursue his interest in this lady in white with the red bandanna and the strawberry milkshake.

"How do you know English so well?" he enquired.

"I lived and worked in America for a year," was her simple explanation.

Heartened to have touched upon another contact point, Colin continued enthusiastically, "I have been to America as well, working as a counsellor in a kids' camp for two successive summers."

Then, wondering where she had come from originally, and anxious to keep the conversation alive, he asked, "And do you live here now?"

"Yes, I live in Krakow," Joanna replied.

"Well maybe you could tell us the best places to see over a weekend," Colin went on, seizing the opportunity to tap into her local knowledge. "We are here until Sunday evening."

"I could indeed. In fact I can show you around the city centre now if you like," Joanna volunteered. She, like most Krakovians, was proud of her beautiful city, and she also found herself strangely attracted to this candid young Irishman.

When Joanna went outside to drink her milkshake and explain to her friends that she was going to show three lads form Ireland around the city, Colin crossed to Ian and Gary and said, "Come on you boys. We're going! This girl is going to show us around!"

When Colin and the other two 'boys' had explained their situation to the New Zealanders and Canadians whom they had been with, all four of them met up outside the cafe.

For the next hour Joanna took great delight in showing the three visitors around the beautiful square, entering and looking around the impressive St. Mary's church, and wandering down the long corridor like inside of the Cloth Hall lined on either side with tidy stalls selling typical Polish souvenirs. Delicate woodcarvings, amber jewellery, table linens, leather goods, they were all there.

When their walking tour of the sights of city centre Krakow was complete the four young people resorted to a chip shop for something to eat.

As they sat there talking, Colin found again that he just could not take his eyes off their exuberant and enchanting tour guide.

Since meeting Joanna his whole emotions had been turned upside down. Neither his heart nor his head seemed to be working as normal. They were both on overdrive. And as for his legs. They felt so hollow that there were times he was sure they were going to let him down completely and leave him in a crumpled heap at her feet!

Is there such a thing as love at first sight? he wondered.

On their way out of the chip shop Colin asked, "Just one more question Joanna. How do we get to the Youth Hostel?"

"Never worry, I will walk you there," Joanna offered. "It is not far, so it would be more difficult to explain than to actually take you round."

"Great," said Colin, and he meant it. That would mean another ten or fifteen minutes with her.

It was surely a positive sign, too, that she wasn't running away. When they had checked into the Youth Hostel, Colin spent some time talking to Joanna. He showed her some photographs of the farm where he lived in Northern Ireland, and his family.

Two things about his photos interested Joanna. The first was the rural nature of them. She loved the sharp black and white contrast on the Friesian cows, the fresh green of the grass and the deep red of the hay sheds. It all seemed so rich and prosperous in a simple country way.

The other point of interest was the people. Having spent ten years painting people into pictures, and having travelled to both the East and the West, Joanna was always fascinated to hear about other people, in other cultures. Looking at those photos Joanna was intrigued to discover that this chap, Colin, had an Aunt Mary and Uncle George. For so had she!

When the photo-viewing session was finished Joanna said, "I must go now but if you don't mind I will have to phone for a taxi. My car is in being repaired and I have to go to another part of town to collect it."

When she had made her phone call, Colin asked, "Would there be any chance of you helping us out on a wee thing in the morning, Joanna? We want to go to Auschwitz Camp in the bus but we haven't a clue where the bus station is. Could you show us?"

"Yes, don't worry. The bus for Auschwitz leaves early. I will meet you here at eight o'clock and take you to the bus station," the lady, still fresh in her white, assured him.

Standing outside, waiting for the taxi, Colin's mind and emotions were even more mixed-up than they had been in the chip shop. He wanted to tell this charming girl how he felt about her.

Should I try to hold her hand?

Should I tell her she is more to me than just a confident and competent city guide?

Should I kiss her Good-night when the taxi comes?

Suddenly all these back of the mind and up from the heart considerations skidded to a halt.

A taxi had pulled up and in two seconds Joanna had opened the door, and called out as she turned to sit down, "This is my taxi. I'm away! See you in the morning."

With that the taxi took off in the direction of the nearest set of traffic lights.

Colin stood gob smacked. She was gone.

And he hadn't asked her for her address. Or even her telephone number.

He knew that she was called Joanna. She had told him her surname as well but he couldn't even say it, not to mention spell it!

He stood staring blankly at the space where the taxi had been.

The taxi which had taken his Joanna away.

Would he ever see her again?

Was she just gone for tonight?

Or was she gone for ever?

27

RED ROSE

Colin needn't have worried.

There had been no need for him to lie awake half the night chiding himself for his crass stupidity. 'I should have sealed that deal last night', he had told himself a billion times in his bunk.

Shortly after eight o'clock Joanna turned up, all bright and breezy at the Youth Hostel. She was still looking every bit as attractive to the fiercely infatuated Colin as she had done twelve hours before.

"Ready?" she enquired, trying to sound ever so matter of fact.

"I brought my car round to take you across to the bus station."

Ready? Of course Colin was ready! And had been since half past six!

Gary and Ian were happy to tag along, too. They appreciated the services of this well-informed and winsome city guide but had just some how begun to question whether Krakow was her only love in this situation.

Time, they knew, would tell.

When all four of them arrived at the bus station, though, there was a problem. Since it was a Saturday both buses to Auschwitz were full. Colin, Ian and Gary couldn't get tickets.

Joanna felt so sorry for them. This was what they had set their hearts on seeing. Now their plans for the day had been thrown into complete disarray. And it was still so early in the morning.

"I tell you what I will do," she offered, prepared to play the role of the awfully kind but sadly badly broke student. "Seeing you can't get on the bus, if you put the petrol in my car, I will take you all to Auschwitz."

Colin's heart skipped a beat. Could he actually believe his ears?

He was going to be given the chance to sit beside this girl-of-his-dreams in her little red Metro all the way to Auschwitz and back! More than a hundred miles!

"Sounds good to me," he remarked.

When they all arrived in the car park at Auschwitz camp in mid-morning Colin was surprised, and not a little disappointed, when Joanna said, "You three go in on your own. I will wait for you here in the car or in the cafe over there. Don't feel you have to hurry back, though. Feel free to take as long as you like."

Colin thought that strange at first. He had honestly begun to believe that Joanna had started to feel a wee spark of something for him too. Why then would she want to drive him and his friends to Auschwitz and not go in to see it with them? Show them around?

As he walked into that Camp and then on around it, however, he began to understand how she felt.

A sign at the entrance, in four different languages, was designed to prepare him, his friends, the two bus loads from Krakow, and the hundreds of others who would visit Auschwitz that day, and on succeeding days, for what they were about to see.

It stated simply:-

'You are entering a place of exceptional horror and tragedy. Please show your respect for those who suffered and died here, behaving in a manner suitable to the dignity of their memory.'

That sign in itself proved enough to subdue the three tearaway lads from Northern Ireland, and as they were introduced to some of the horrors of what they saw variously described as 'a factory of death' and 'the world's largest graveyard,' Colin began to appreciate why Joanna had chosen to remain in her car.

Many thousands of the victims of that place had been ordinary, honest Polish people.

Her people.

It would have been altogether too painful for her to come in. It was in fact unspeakably brave of her to even volunteer to bring them here.

Was there, perhaps, another reason for her wanting to help them? And him, particularly?

Or was he merely clutching at straws ...?

On the journey back north towards Krakow Colin asked Joanna to stop a number of times. Being a country boy at heart he wanted to take photographs of the animals they saw. And particularly the horses at work in the fields. To Colin they were the epitome of both silent power and rural peace.

He had another fixation for his photography, too, and that was the numerous quaint country churches. Many of them were beautiful and he repeatedly asked their chauffeur to stop while he took his pictures.

Joanna was quite happy to comply with his requests but what struck her as uncanny after their fourth or fifth church stop was that every single church they stopped at seemed to have a wedding taking place in it!

And when they arrived back in Krakow and walked back up to the Market Square and into the stately St. Mary's Church there was a wedding in it as well!

To Joanna this had become more than a strange coincidence. Was her wish on shooting star night about to be fulfilled? Her prayer answered?

No, she told herself, these were only three fetching and fun loving foreigners, but on the other hand the manner in which Colin had grabbed her hand and marched her down the aisle after that wedding to the still-playing recessional music was possibly more than fun ....

Time, she knew, would tell.

Later that afternoon, after they had all had tea together, Ian and Gary declared themselves 'very tired' and returned to the Hostel. They by that time could sense that a certain chemistry was developing between their friend and their guide so they decided to make themselves scarce. They had 'played gooseberry' long enough.

Colin was in his element. He now had this lovely girl all to himself.

They walked idly round the city with Joanna pointing out more of the sights ... Wawel Castle, imposing on its hill overlooking the River Vistula, Wawel Cathedral with its golden dome, the Florianska Gate with all the artists showing their paintings ...

This gave Joanna an idea.

"Perhaps you and Ian and Gary would like to come around to my studio and see some of my work," she suggested. "We will pass the Hostel on the way back to the car. You could call in and ask them."

Colin said that he would very much like to see her studio and her paintings, but when he went into the Hostel to pass on the invitation to his two friends, he never quite made their bedroom! He stopped on the first landing, waited an appropriate length of time, then went out and told their kind would-be hostess, "No, the lads are still very tired. They won't be coming!"

How could he look at them all evening, when he had the opportunity to spend a few more hours on his own with this angel?

On arriving in Joanna's studio Colin was taken aback completely. Absolutely amazed. Totally thunderstruck.

The whole living area was littered with paintings in various stages of completion. Big ones, small ones, striking ones, sombre ones ... Colin had never up until that moment taken much of an interest in things artistic. Having been raised on a farm he knew more about bullocks than backgrounds, and more about pigs than perspective.

But this art was stunning. It held him spellbound.

He was reduced to stammering out a feeble, "Did you do all this, Joanna?"

"Yes," came the almost shy reply. "Why?"

"Because it's brilliant!" he exclaimed, beginning to wonder what sort of a gem this was he had stumbled upon. Her quiet reticence to enter Auschwitz, and now this roomful of impressive paintings.

This girl was both tender and talented.

'What am I doing sitting here?" he wondered.

His reverie was broken by Joanna offering to show him some photographs of her family.

"There are some photos there you might like to look at while I tidy up a few things," she said, handing him over two folders, both slightly the worse for the wear.

As Colin flicked through them he passed as quickly as was courteous over people whom he didn't know posing in places he didn't know, but there were some he lingered over for some time. And those were the photographs of this girl whom he had just discovered was a gifted artist.

There was one in particular at which he stopped and held it in his hand for ages. Mesmerized.

It was a head and shoulders portrait of Joanna, taken outside at sunset. The orange-red hues in the sky gave her face a beautiful warm glow. Her eyes sparkled. She had the ever-present string, short this time, of coloured beads around her neck.

Colin now had another point confirmed to him. Something he thought he already knew.

In addition to being both tender and talented, in his estimation this girl was really beautiful.

Suddenly subconsciously aware that he had spent a disproportionate length of time over that one particular picture, he flipped it to the bottom of his pile, skimmed through the rest, and looking up returned the two packs to Joanna.

"Those are great," he said, and then, afraid of being questioned on them, proceeded to change the subject.

"There is a lovely fragrance in here. What's that Joanna?" he enquired.

"It's probably the apples," his hostess suggested. "I bought some fresh apples yesterday." And it was then that her guest noticed a large bowl of crisp red apples on the table.

"Yes that's what it is," Colin conceded. "I love the smell of apples."

"We have pears too," Joanna joked. "But they are still out there in my neighbour's garden. On the tree."

Then not even waiting for her new friend's response she went on, "Would you like a pear, Colin? Come on! The neighbours are away and they told me to help myself!"

By the time he could rise from the chair Joanna was out the back door, through the fence into her neighbour's garden, and over below the pear tree.

Colin dutifully followed.

It had come to the stage with him that he was so besotted with this vibrant young lady that he would follow her anywhere!

By the time he reached her Joanna had picked up three windfall pears.

"Come on, help yourself Colin!" she invited.

Colin did as he was told. He helped himself to five big juicy pears.

Within minutes the young couple had settled themselves on the neighbour's seat in the neighbour's garden to eat the neighbour's pears.

From where they were sitting they could see the moon through the pear tree, its face shredded into sharp black wrinkles by the upper branches.

As he bit into his second pear, and the juice spurted everywhere, Colin quipped, "What a romantic meal for two!"

This young romantic had more on his mind than eating pears, however.

Joanna could feel his other arm slithering slowly down over the back of the seat and down around her shoulder … She somehow wasn't ready for that, though.

Holding hands in a crowded church was one thing, but arms around in an isolated garden was quite another.

Jumping up, she raced back through the fence, calling after her as she went, "Let's have more tea!"

Now the last thing Colin wanted or needed was more tea, and when he had arrived back in her kitchen and was wiping the pear juice off himself, he told her so.

"To tell you the truth Joanna," he said. "I don't need any more tea!"

"Why don't we go out again then, now that it's dark?" she suggested.

"There is something else I want to show you!"

Colin couldn't understand what it was that she wanted to show him after dark that she couldn't show him during the day, but they both went out into the car and set off.

After having driven for about a mile through city streets Joanna parked the car and said, "This is where we get out."

Joanna walked away, talking away. And Colin was also quite happy to walk away with her, talking away to her.

When they reached a steep incline Joanna side stepped behind her friend and placed her hands over his eyes.

"Keep on walking!" she whispered tersely.

When he felt her cold hands, with their long strong fingers, over his eyes Colin was ready to obey any command. It wasn't as good as holding hands had been, nor as good as arms around in the orchard could have been, but at least it was contact. And one had to be thankful for anything!

Suddenly Joanna barked another command. "Stop!" When obeyed, this was followed by another, "Now look!"

His captor had, all in one movement, removed the blinding hands, allowing Colin to view the panorama stretching out below him.

It was breathtaking.

Regardless of what direction one looked there was always something to see. The twinkling lights of the entire city of Krakow stretched out away into the distance of the clear moonlit night …

Colin didn't want that enchanting evening to end.

But it had to, and Joanna left him off at the Hostel promising to pick Colin and his two friends up in the morning for 'a trip up into the mountains', explaining to them that she had a standing invitation to visit two of her friends who lived there.

This time, though, Colin had no doubts about the arrangement.

He just knew Joanna would tum up that Sunday morning.

He felt that she felt almost the same way about him as he felt about her.

Time, he knew, would tell.

And Joanna did arrive outside the Youth hostel next morning, dead on time. To take Colin, Ian and Gary on a trip up into the mountains.

What a day that turned out to be, also.

They drove up to a mountain retreat owned by Joanna's friends.

There the three youth hostellers were introduced to Mark and his wife Bozena, and they all had lunch.

To both Colin and Joanna that trip into the beautiful mountain scenery with its shining lakes and endless green forests was special, for by now they had only eyes for each other.

It was also a day, though, overshadowed by an increasingly gloomy cloud hanging over the both of them. For they knew that Colin was booked to leave Krakow that evening, on the ten thirty five train to Vienna.

When that dreaded time came Ian and Gary went on into an empty compartment, assuring Colin that they would keep him a seat but warning him not to miss the train!

So this was it.

The parting of the ways.

Neither of the two of them knew what to do, or say, now. Or next. Or first. Or last.

There was a silence, the silence of two hearts at one, and neither of them able to express precisely how they felt.

Then Joanna broke the deadlock.

She leant forward and gave Colin that sign he had been looking for all weekend.

Instinctively, impulsively, she kissed him on the cheek.

The lad whose whole emotions she had turned upside down and inside out in the space of forty-eight hours, needed no second prompt.

He lifted Joanna clean off her feet, swung her round in a complete circle on the station platform, and planted a big kiss on her lips before planting her feet back on the ground.

The guard blew his whistle.

"I will have to go," Colin panted.

"Don't go yet, I have something for you!" Joanna said, slipping something into his hand.

"And I have something for you too!" he replied and reaching into the inner pocket of the jacket he was wearing, presented her with a single red rose.

That was his seal. His token of affection.

Colin climbed aboard and almost immediately, in a clank of metal, the train pulled away.

Rushing to the nearest corridor window he slid it open and waved and waved to the solitary figure standing waving back from the platform.

Then, before he joined his two friends in the compartment, he looked down at what he had in his hand. What had his angel of light given him?

A tear welled up in his eye when he saw what it was.

It was the photograph he had dwelt so long over in Joanna's studio the previous evening, and the beautiful subject had written her name and address on the back!

It was now Joanna's turn to stare into empty space.

She stood for another five minutes on the platform, rooted to the spot, staring down the silent line. Tears glistened on her cheeks, too.

Suddenly she was gripped by an irresistible conviction.

A voice in her inner being, that inner being which had once been fraught with doubts and darkness, but was now illuminated by the light of the love and guidance of God, said clearly and unequivocally, "You have met your future husband."

And she believed it.

Another impulse overcame her.

She lifted up her partly-crushed, full-petalled, single red rose. And kissed it.

The deal was sealed.

28

PRAISE THE LORD!
I'M YOUR MAN

That was a busy autumn.

Poland had been for Colin one of the first stops on a ten week tour of Europe. He wasn't planning to be back home in N. Ireland until mid-November.

Late September saw Joanna launched into her most hectic year at University. It was her fifth and final year, and in addition to her normal studies she was also teaching painting in the Deaf and Dumb Institute and was obliged to provide her sponsors with a range of paintings by June 1994.

At different times during his travels, Colin thought back to that wonderful weekend in Krakow. Will I ever see that beautiful girl again? he asked himself, every time he thought of her.

In reflective moments in her studio Joanna also remembered those three fantastic days, the red rose and the crushing conviction that she had met her future husband.

By early December, however, with the chill of winter upon her, she began to think that perhaps she had been mistaken.

Perhaps it had only been a flight of fancy.

Shooting stars, ships sailing north, Ireland, a lovable lad with winning ways ...

Perhaps she had just turned overly soppy and sentimental. Then came the Christmas card from Colin.

It was a specially chosen one.

'Just For You'.

Joanna was thrilled. And, remembering his love of animals, and particularly horses, returned a card of Krakow, with a pony on it.

Just for him.

Colin was thrilled. And in February Joanna received a Valentine's card from him, covered with all kinds of one-verse love stuff.

Just for her.

Then, as his love for Joanna grew, Colin was faced with an emotional, mental, and spiritual dilemma. Every time he thought of her, and with each of the cards he had written to her, he realised increasingly that he wanted to be with her, and only her, always.

The problem was that he was a Christian and he had already invited this light of his life over to spend the summer holiday with his family in Northern Ireland. But he had no idea where she stood spiritually.

What would happen, for instance, if she turned out to be a Communist?

It didn't bear thinking about!

In his first full letter to her, Colin determined to tell Joanna of his faith. Let her know what he believed. She probably wouldn't understand one single word of what he was writing about, but he decided that he must tell her. Whatever the cost.

He had heard often in church, and had read it in the Bible, about 'not being unequally yoked together with unbelievers'. And for years he had believed it.

Now he was set to be tested on it. He was developing an obsessive love for a beautiful, talented Polish girl.

What would he do if she proved to be an 'unbeliever'?

Or what would he do if she never answered his letter? If she concluded that he was some kind of an Irish religious nut and decided to unscrew him out of her life?

That certainly didn't bear thinking about either!

One Sunday evening after church he decided he had to do it. Write to Joanna. Put her in the picture, before this loving relationship progressed any farther.

So he wrote, weighing every word:-

'21 March, 1994.

Dear Joanna,

'It's now 12.00 midnight and the first day of British Summer Time is just over. It's a beautiful night with a full moon, so quiet and peaceful. There is a lovely light and frost covering the ground.

'Today is Sunday. I'm just back from church a couple of hours ago. I go to church every Sunday, morning and night. I enjoy it very much.

'I became a Christian when I was 17 years old. To do this I simply accepted Jesus into my life by prayerfully saying, 'Into my heart, into my heart, come into my heart Lord Jesus. Come in today, come in to stay, come into my heart Lord Jesus'. By doing this my sins were washed away and my night was turned to day, since Jesus came into my heart.

'I now own Him as my Lord and Saviour. He's my best friend. I give Him all my problems and pray to Him often.

'It is a nice feeling, a personal love for me which I thought I should share with you …

'I will go now, and love and leave you. Please take care of yourself and write again to me soon. Every day when I come home I check the post for mail, especially from Poland. May God bless you wherever you go,

'Till we meet again,

'Loads of love,

'Colin.'

On Monday Colin posted his letter, and then waited and waited and waited. The first week wasn't too bad but after that he was back to looking for letters every day as soon as he came home from work. So great did the suspense become that he often phoned his mother in his lunch hour with some petty excuse, only to ask, as casually as he could, before replacing the receiver, "Any mail for me today?"

But none seemed to come.

March gave way to April, Easter came and went, and still nothing.

Had he spoilt it all? Had the testimony been too much?

Would he never see another Polish stamp?

Had he seen his last Krakow postmark?

Still the days went on.

Had he been a fool to paint such a simple picture of salvation to such a gifted artist?

Then it came.

And when it did Colin could barely believe it for he had himself convinced that he had blown the whole relationship sky-high, trying to justify his actions to his breaking heart by telling it that what he had done was 'the right thing'.

Now a letter from Poland. With a Krakow postmark. Joanna's writing…

Without stopping to eat anything or even speak to anybody he rushed to his bedroom to read it.

Would Joanna have understood what he was writing about? Or was this her last ever letter?

When with trembling, fumbling hands he eventually succeeded in ripping open the envelope, he saw that the letter consisted of three sheets of writing paper, one gold and two white, all closely written on, both sides.

That, in itself, was encouraging.

This was no half-page 'Dear Colin Thanks but no thanks letter', either.

Then as he began to read the letter Colin was absolutely dumbfounded. What Joanna had written half way down the second side of the gold page left the hands holding the letter trembling.

Some minor problems with grammatical construction of her second language only served to add to the sincerity of her sentiment.

The love-struck lad was astounded to read:-

'You tell me in your last letter that you became a Christian when you were 17 years old. That's great that praying to Jesus gives you so much. The time we spend with Jesus is so important. He is the one to whom we can believe to, and we can follow to. He is the only one and the best to follow his example.

'I had a long way to go to find him. You can't be only Christian by name. "You must be Christian by heart.

'My story is pretty long. I'd like to tell you when I see you. It is so very much important to me.

'For a few years I totally lost the way to Jesus.

'I couldn't find him. I felt very bad with that.

'Sometimes I didn't think of it. Sometimes I almost cried.

'I started to feel a very painful wound in my heart.

'Then somewhere on the horizon I saw the light. I started to move towards it, though I still had so many doubts.

'I was meeting some friends, talking to them about it. I asked them to pray for me, because I still doubted and still did not understand how good is Jesus, our Lord.

'It took a long, long time and suddenly one day came. One of my friends came to visit me and we prayed together at my home. I felt exactly what I must do. I felt I must invite Jesus into my heart. I felt I need him like nothing else.

'And that was it!

'I will tell you some more about it. I hope it will be very soon. I already would like to be in Ireland ...'

Colin stopped reading there.

He began to shake all over. Not only hands were going now. Arms, legs, every part of his body had been affected.

Could this possibly be true?

The one girl he had met and liked so much, in a large city, in a foreign country, was a Christian?

Impulsively he dashed along the hallway, a rent open envelope and a sheet of gold paper in one hand, two white pages in the other.

When he entered the living room, his father and mother were both sitting waiting for him to come down and join them for the evening meal.

There was a brother or two about. There was always a brother or two about, for Colin had six of them. No sisters. Just six brothers.

He was about to explode with excitement. Addressing his parents he exclaimed, "Guess what?! Remember the girl I was talking to you about from Poland? Joanna? Remember? Well she's a Christian!"

Then, without even waiting to gauge his parents reaction, which he knew would be good anyway, he belted back along the hall yelling at the top of his voice, "Praise the Lord! I'm your man! Praise the Lord! I'm your man!"

When he arrived back, breathless, in his bedroom, he seated himself on the edge of the bed, still all aquiver. There was just one more thing he had to do before going down to dinner.

And that was read the rest of the letter!

29

LET'S WAIT UNTIL
THE LIGHT ERUPTS

At seven o'clock one Sunday morning in early May, long before time for church, Joanna drove down to Wawel Castle for a walk.

Having parked her car she walked a short distance through the Planty, then up the old cobbled pavement towards the ancient castle. The scent from the magnificent magnolia trees with their tulip-like blossoms hung heavy on the early morning.

Spring was in the air.

And spring was in Joanna's heart.

Half-way up the slope to the castle she stopped and gazed down over the wall towards the River Vistula which was beginning to glint in the after-sunrise sunlight. Then, directing her attention to the path directly below the castle ramparts and along the bank of the river, she was pleasantly surprised to discover that there were two other people besides herself out at that early hour.

An elderly couple were sitting on one of the still dew damp benches holding crumpled bags of crushed bread in wrinkled hands.

Torn-off lump by torn-off lump they were feeding the pigeons which flapped and fought around their feet.

It all seemed so peaceful …

Joanna thought of Colin, and of the date.

It was the eighth of May, and the eighth of May was Colin's birthday.

She stared fixedly down at the patient pigeon-feeders bathed in light, and wondered if the day would ever come when she and Colin would be able to sit together like that? Wherever they wanted? And for as long as they liked?

They were, at least, taking the first steps towards achieving that objective. In recent letters they had been discussing Joanna's much anticipated summer visit to Dundrod, County Antrim.

However, before that occurred there was something else, another imminent and important matter, to which she must give her undivided attention.

Tomorrow, Monday 9th May, 1994, was the day on which she had to conduct 'the defence of her diploma". She had to present her year's art work before the leading professors of the University of Fine Arts to have it assessed for her Master of Arts degree.

There was much to do. And think about.

Future plans for faraway places would have to be placed on hold for the present.

On Monday morning Joanna went early to the Krakow Cultural Centre close to the Market Square, for it was there she had mounted her paintings for her diploma, and it was there that she had to make her presentation.

For her diploma, and for her sponsors, Joanna had completed ninety-nine paintings, each on a square of rough canvas, and each with a narrow rectangular picture painted on the square, leaving unpainted canvas on either side.

The idea was that each central rectangular strip represented a door with the artist on the outside, looking in at the various representations of life and figures within. Joanna imagined herself as having had a new beginning, as having stepped out of the picture to look back and reflect on life as she had known it. This fanciful pictorial portrayal of experience was worked in all the colours of the rainbow. Some of these colours were strong and bright and stark, others pale and muted.

The purpose of the 'defence' was to allow a final year student to explain the theme or purpose of his or her paintings, not just the medium or method by which they had been done. Some students had ponderous files of notes for this occasion, fully aware that they would only be permitted to present a small proportion of them as the examining professors couldn't possibly hear it all.

Joanna had decided to adopt a different approach.

Rather than make her presentation in a monotonous spiel of artistic jargon she wrote a poem, which she spent that last-minute Monday morning time writing out in script, mounting, and placing on an easel, before a window. This allowed the rays of light from the window to shine through the white paper on which the poem had been transcribed.

At eleven o'clock the University professors and a number of Joanna's friends gathered in the room in the Cultural Centre where she had mounted her exhibition.

They were all awaiting her 'defence'.

Joanna began by pointing to her pictures neatly mounted in rows on the wall. "These are my ninety-nine paintings, and I should like to explain them by reading you a poem which I have written. It is called, 'In A Hundred Places There Is Beginning.'"

A puzzled look crossed the faces of some of her audience. Some of them wondered, 'Ninety-nine paintings, one hundred places ... Has this student made some sort of a mistake? Or is she just a better artist that a mathematician?!'

Some were puzzled, but not all. Professor Krupinski, her supervisor, sat with a knowing smile on his face.

Everyone sat spellbound as she began reading ...

In A Hundred Places There Is ...

Beginning.
Silence that comes without reason ...
Space touched here and there
with inner trails
bright with the sounds of universe.

White breath
Yellow breath
Red breath
Blue breath
Green breath
A breath that's black

A breath of black
A breath of green
A breath of blue
A breath of red
A breath of yellow
A breath of white

A hundred breaths pray inside me.
Feel, how your breath expands the space.
The light grows, it takes away your breath ...

Let us free ourselves of the darkness of the world
into which we were thrown.
Let's not explain, let's look.
Let's wait
until
the light erupts.

Let us get plaited in the spokes of a fiery wheel
Let's rise with light
Let's leave with light ...

A hundred pictures
A hundred breaths
A hundred spaces
A hundred passages

A hundred mirrors
A hundred revelations
A hundred thoughts

In a hundred places there is still

a beginning.

Joanna paused for breath when she had finished reading her poem. A
curious hush had descended on the company.
Glances flitted from the ninety-nine paintings on the wall, whose

Joanna and her art

Exhibition at One Oxford Street Gallery in Belfast in summer 1994

Amish inspiration in USA 1996

Diploma Exhibition in Hilton Hotel, Germany, with art sponsor, Mr. Geers in 1994

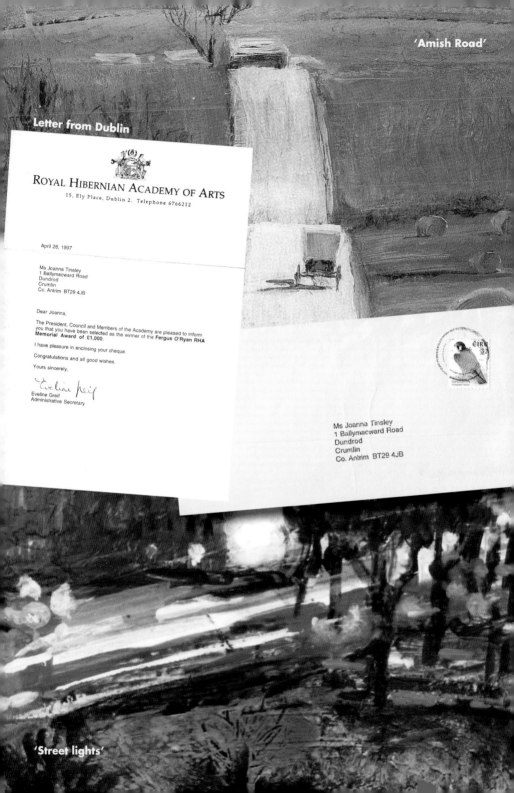

'Amish Road'

Letter from Dublin

ROYAL HIBERNIAN ACADEMY OF ARTS

15, Ely Place, Dublin 2. Telephone 6766212

April 28, 1997

Ms Joanna Tinsley
1 Ballymacward Road
Dundrod
Crumlin
Co. Antrim BT29 4JB

Dear Joanna,

The President, Council and Members of the Academy are pleased to inform you that you have been selected as the winner of the **Fergus O'Ryan RHA Memorial Award of £1,000.**

I have pleasure in enclosing your cheque.

Congratulations and all good wishes.

Yours sincerely,

Eveline Greif
Administrative Secretary

ÉIRE 32

Ms Joanna Tinsley
1 Ballymacward Road
Dundrod
Crumlin
Co. Antrim BT29 4JB

'Street lights'

Charles
Gillmore
Gallery
Exhibition
1997

Joanna Tinsley
Solo Exhibition
James Gallery
Dalkey
From June 17th

RAC

Exhibition
advertised
in Dublin in
1998

Painting in Donegal

Exhibition in Mount Stewart 1996

Article from 'Northern Woman' magazine, October 1999

My Favourite Room

PHOTOGRAPHS
GEORGE ROE, BELFAST

ARTISTIC LICENCE

Ali Fell reports

Jo Tinsley is Northern Ireland's most sought after female contemporary artist.

Her studio is built alongside her mobile home, moored in the yard of her husband's family's farmhouse near Stoneyford. There are windows on three sides, overlooking fields on one side, and a neighbour's garden, a "mini Mount Stewart," on the other.

The quiet is punctuated by the sound of a nearby stream and the crowing of her bantam hens. A rural paradise, these are ideal surroundings for the artist from Kraków in Poland.

"I have always been very inspired by nature; there is very little that I like that is man-made," she says. "My studio has such lovely big windows, it is very open to nature. And you can't see any buildings. I also appreciate my privacy a lot, and this is very private."

An unconventional home, Jo and husband Colin chose the mobile at first out of convenience. Jo adds: "We both love to travel, and this gives us a feeling of our lives being a holiday.

"I like to shop when I travel and bring things home to use in my house, and I have a few things from home – little hand-made things."

Although she is not sure that they will make a permanent home here, Jo does enjoy life in Northern Ireland. "I find the light here very inspiring. It is so changeable, you can sometimes see it change as it moves across the fields, making everything look so different. Perhaps that is why there are so many artists here.

JO TINSLEY
Q&A

Favourite shop:
Anywhere and everywhere, from Moroccan tea-pot shops, to traditional Polish woodcarvers, to Egyptian baskets weavers.

Most treasured item:
A hexagonal piece of hand-blown glass from a church tower in Kraków. She received it as a birthday gift when the windows were replaced by modern double glazing. It hangs in the window of her studio, and reminds her of home, and the rocks at the Giant's Causeway.

Best bargain:
Artists own work, available from Charles Gilmore Galleries, Holywood. Prices range from £500 to £4,000.

Painting together with Joanna's Polish nephew Janek during his holidays in N. Ireland

'Moonlight Iceskaters'

Finishing 'Fashion Show'

In the studio painting
'Fashion Show'

Joanna's solo
exhibition in
The James
Gallery in 2006

'Self portrait' as an Amish girl

Painting in Australia

'Amish children'
February 2006

'Lady with umbrella-self portrait',
September 2007

Exhibition in Dublin 2008

'Lady with umbrella'

'Chatting in the Hay field'

'Swiss celebration'

'Sheep by the moonlight'

Belfast Castle - celebrating after art exhibition

Mayor of Lisburn James Tinsley, Joanna, Arts Minister Edwin Poots beside 'The joy of the summer'

With older brother Thomas who surprised Joanna! September 2007

With younger brother Maciek, October 2007

In front of the gallery just after exhibition

Paintings in Joanna's
studio ready for February 2008
show in Dublin

Painting 'Birthday girl'

CHARLES GILMORE GALLERIES
HOLYWOOD

NEW WORKS BY
JOANNA TINSLEY

Commissioned portrait of children, 9x3 feet size!

Joanna in the studio

In front of Merchant Hotel in Belfast, after visiting her exhibition in the gallery of the hotel

MERCHANT HOTEL

Colin & Joanna

purpose they now partly understood, to the easel with the handwritten poem, which they had just heard read, to the reader, her face now flushed a rich glowing red to match the rich glowing red of the ribbon tying up her hair.

Sensing their expectancy, and since no one else had dared interrupt something so sensitive, she continued, "I know what you will all be asking yourselves. 'There are only nine-nine paintings here. Ninety-nine beginnings. Where is the one hundredth beginning?'"

She paused, to acknowledge the slowly nodding heads.

Then proceeded to answer her original question, by asking more. "Is it in the house? No!

"Is it already in some gallery somewhere? No!

"Is it still in my studio, not yet finished? No!

"I tell you. No! No! No!

"It is not there on that wall, either.

"It was not done with oils on canvas.

The one hundredth beginning is right here. It is in my heart!"

There was an awesome, almost reverent silence as Joanna sat down.

Normally at the defence of a diploma the examining Professors would be lining up to put questions to the candidate.

In Joanna's case that didn't happen.

There was just silence. Absolute, total, silence.

It seemed as though nobody wanted to be first to crack his way out of the cocoon of calm which had engulfed them all.

Eventually, after two minutes, which seemed like two hours, Joanna's Professor of Painting stood up, and in the absence of any further comment, addressed his fellow-professors, and her fellow students.

"Ladies and gentlemen," he began, slowly, obviously measuring his words. "I feel we ought to award this student the Laurel Wreath, not only for her art and her poetry, but also for her thinking. When she submitted her poem to me two weeks ago for approval, I have to admit that I was touched. I felt that there was something strangely spiritual about it, for not only did I realise that this poem was an excellent expression of the purpose of her paintings but I also recognise in it a depth of personal experience…"

Having completed his summing up he turned to Joanna and addressed her personally, making the announcement, everyone was waiting to hear.

"Miss Maciantowicz , I am pleased to award you the Degree of Master of Arts, Grade A."

The silence was soon shattered after that! The small room rang to loud cheers and applause.

Many from Joanna's family and her University friends rushed forward to congratulate her. Flowers were pushed into her hand.

Joanna Maciantowicz M.A. was overwhelmed by a Marvellous sense of Achievement. There was an indescribable feeling of relief and release after all the tensed-up weeks and months of preparation.

When everyone who wanted to speak to her had spoken to her, Joanna led them out of the Cultural Centre. She then ran into the Market Square, where, much to the amusement of the ambling tourists, she threw up her arms and exclaimed, "I'm free! I'm free!"

There was an eruption of pigeons following that explosion of peace.

'Let's wait

'until

'the light erupts' was how she had stated it.

In her own 'defence'.

30

I WAS ONLY PULLIN' YOUR LEG!

Having graduated from University, Joanna had to fulfil her commitment to GEERS, her sponsors. Within the space of one month she was required to have her complete set of ninety-nine paintings, plus some others, transported to Dresden in Germany, and hung in the gallery of the Hilton Hotel there. And that was not all. She also had to arrange for a catalogue to be printed describing her work. When she did this she entitled the pamphlet, 'In Hundred Places ...' including within it her poem which had attracted such academic acclaim both on the day of her 'defence' and afterwards.

Thus May was another hectic but happy month.

For Joanna knew that after she had mounted her exhibition in Dresden she would be free for the remainder of the summer. And she had plans for that!

In early June Bertha's father loaded all his daughter's paintings and most of Joanna's into his van and all three of them set out for the trip across Poland and into Germany. Joanna travelled in her own car which she had packed with her remaining paintings plus clothes and art materials.

She was well prepared to stay away for three months. Not in Dresden, though!

The official opening of the exhibition, 'In Hundred Places ...' was held on Wednesday 8th June, 1994. It was a formal affair, presided over by Anne Burghardt, manager of the Hilton gallery, and Mr. Wolfgang Geers, chairman of the sponsoring company.

For a week after the opening of her exhibition Joanna remained in the German city, seeing the sights, attending the gallery. But a week was all she felt she could stay.

She had love in her heart and a long journey to make.

In the middle of the following week she packed her little red Metro again, and set off, not back to Krakow, though. Since she was halfway there anyway she reasoned that she may as well continue all the way west across Germany into France, and over to Calais on the coast.

Thus the adventure of a lifetime for the lovestruck Polish painter began.

At the port of Calais Joanna bought a one way Land bridge ticket to Northern Ireland. She was determined to get there, and if and when she did, she didn't care if or when she came back. All she wanted to do was see Colin again, and be with him.

Since each of them had discovered that the other was a Christian, an invisible, but infinite, bond seemed to be pulling them irresistibly together. Early in the evening of Friday 17th June the telephone rang in the Tinsley home in Dundrod.

When Colin's mum answered it she was somewhat taken aback initially to hear a woman's voice, speaking English with a funny foreign twang, enquiring, "Hello. Is that Mrs. Tinsley?"

"Yes, it is. That's me," she replied, slowly, almost cautiously. "Well, this is Joanna," came the lilting voice from the other end of the line. "I am ringing from London. Is Colin there, please?"

"Yes, indeed he is!" Elizabeth Tinsley went on in totally different tone, realising that this was the girl Colin had been telling them all about, about fifty times a day! "Hold on and I will fetch him for you!"

Back in a telephone kiosk in London Joanna's heart had skipped a beat. She had made contact with Colin's home and his mum had sounded so warm and welcoming. Her rich Northern Ireland accent sounded like happy chirping birds to Joanna. It was a powerful tonic to a tiring traveller.

In thirty seconds Colin had picked up the receiver.

He was absolutely thrilled to hear Joanna's voice again. Although they had begun to correspond more regularly, the loving pair had never actually spoken to each other since the parting on the platform last September.

For months Colin had been planning all the lovely loving things he was going to say to his lady in white the first time they had a chance to speak again in person. This, though, was not quite how he had imagined it would be!

Since it was evening, all the Tinsleys were at home. Every single one of them. So Colin was conscious of eight pairs of eyes watching him, and eight pairs of ears listening to him on his first opportunity to talk to his beautiful girl from Poland for the first time in nine months.

The telephone call was brief, and to the point. Joanna was in a booth with a limited amount of change but a mighty message. What it amounted to was that she hoped to travel northwards through England on Saturday, and depending on progress hoped to cross from Stranraer to Larne sometime on Sunday, and be with him later that day.

Just after Joanna had said, "Must go now Colin, my money's finished. Love you!" there was a click and the receiver in his hand began to hum with the dialling tone.

She was gone!

And what had he said?

Something about, "Is it not awful dear to phone from there where you are?!"

How romantic!

Colin stood for a few minutes in a stupor. His Joanna was coming to see him in two days time. She would be here sometime on Sunday!

And he hadn't yet had a chance to breathe one word of all those lovely loving things that had been bursting out of his heart for months!

Sunday morning was not an ideal time of the week for a stranger to find her way around Northern Ireland, for there were very few people out and about on the roads. However, using a road map, Joanna arrived in the Dundrod district. And then the fun began. She started asking the few people whom she did manage to find, where Ballymacward Road was. Most of them just stared at her blankly. They either didn't understand her standard English with a foreign accent, or else they genuinely didn't know where it was but most of them told her with a friendly smile that they had never heard of it!

Eventually, though, Joanna discovered a marvellously enlightened gentleman who was able to tell her it was 'round here somewhere,' but he wasn't 'just sure how to get to it'.

So she drove on, and quite by chance discovered it herself. There it was. On the sign at the end of a road. 'Ballymacward Road'.

And it wasn't too difficult to find number one either. She would try the first farm along the road.

As she drove in the farm gate Joanna felt satisfied. Fulfilled. Here she was at last.

All that remained was for her to ring the doorbell. She would soon be in Colin's arms.

Meanwhile Colin had been waiting for her.

He had been up early to check the calving cows. In fact the cows were checked more often that Sunday morning than any cows had ever been. For Colin wanted to be out about the yard when Joanna arrived.

In and out, in and out. Still no red Metro.

Then he decided he would have a quick bath and change for church and if his expected guest hadn't arrived before eleven o'clock he might just go. He didn't like to miss the morning service. And she might not arrive until the afternoon. Or maybe even later on than that …

At half-past ten Joanna rang the doorbell, and a young man came to the door.

"Excuse me," she said, looking tired and travel-worn, "is this one Ballymacward Road? I am looking for the home of the Tinsley family."

The lad at the door looked ever so serious. "Yes," he admitted, "this is the Ballymacward Road, but no, there are no Tinsleys live around here. Tinsley … Tinsley …Tinsley …" he went on repeating the name as though he had just heard it for the first time in his life. "No, sorry, there is nobody with that name around these parts!"

Joanna was bamboozled.

She was sure she had found number one, Ballymacward Road, the address she had written so often on her letters to Colin. And the lad-at-the-door looked remarkably like Colin, too. But he had definitely said there were 'no Tinsleys round here'.

Turning slowly, her heart dropped down into her specially worn white shoes, she whispered, "Sorry. There must be some mistake."

What was she going to do now? She had crossed Poland, Germany, France, The English Channel, England, Scotland, The Irish Sea, and it seemed like the half of Northern Ireland. The sign had said that this was the Ballymacward Road but this chap had definitely said there were 'no Tinsleys round here …'

Pitying her obvious dejection the young man on the step called after her, "Jo? Are you Jo? Is it Colin you are looking for? Sorry, I was only pull'n' your leg!" Joanna made a sudden about turn. The chap on the step was Colin's brother James. He was beaming from ear to ear.

As she walked back towards the door again Joanna saw James get roughly bundled out of the way.

Colin had arrived.

He had just been stepping out of the bath when he heard the doorbell.

Without even taking time to dry himself he started to pull on his clothes. His shirt had insisted in sticking like glue to every inch of his still-wet body. Socks had been pulled on over wet feet. There was no need to bother about shoes.

His hair was half-dried and standing on end. He hadn't been able to locate a comb in the confusion.

In two seconds Colin had begun where he had left off.

He picked Joanna up, swung her round, and planted a kiss on her lips before planting her feet on the ground!

It was almost too good to be true, the lady in white had returned!

Joanna was dressed as he had seen her on that very first September day. White blouse, white trousers, white shoes.

Marvellous! Marvellous! Marvellous!

Colin missed church that morning. He had to show Joanna to her room, help her unload her car, and then take her for a long, long walk around the farm

By the end of that day Joanna had been introduced to all the family and felt immediately at home amongst them. There was a genuine warmth about these sincere Christian people to which she found it easy to respond.

And on Monday evening she was to see Colin at work on the farm.

He was working out in the fields for the most of the evening, helping with the segregation and T.B. testing of both cows and calves. Half way through the afternoon he looked down at himself. His overalls were covered in cow dung. He even had it on his hands and in his hair! It was just one of those days.

Every time he got a chance he looked across at the gate. At least Joanna was still there. She hadn't headed back to Poland yet. She had been telling him yesterday about her exhibition in The Hilton Hotel somewhere in Germany, and here she was now watching him coping with cows! How desperately ordinary!

What on earth would she think? Would she last until the weekend or would she head for home on Wednesday?

What he didn't know was that she thought he was wonderful! One of the cows tried to run away once and Colin grabbed it by the head, stuck his finger and thumb in its nostrils and brought it slithering to a halt. How brave he was! And how very, very strong he must be!

All the farmer's son had done was grab the animal by the pressure point inside the nostril and exert pressure with the finger and thumb and it had to stop.

As they walked back to the farmhouse Colin wondered that this gifted artist would choose to be anywhere near him.

He looked, and smelt, like the midden!

Later on that summer's evening Colin and Joanna went walking again. The cowhand was all cleaned up by then and it was one of those balmy evenings when everyone wants to be out, enjoying the countryside.

Joanna was full of questions about the country and the country way of life.

It was pleasant. Relaxed. Idyllic.

They were almost back at the farmhouse when they stopped at a bridge. Colin jumped up, sat on the parapet, turned round and with undue force speared the piece of grass he had been sucking into the stream below.

Although Joanna didn't realise it for a moment or two, all that uncharacteristic exaggerated behaviour was a build up to the question he had planned to ask her. It was something he had wanted to put to her in person, so had never written it in a letter.

"Joanna, will you be my girl-friend?" he enquired.

The love which was bursting out of his heart overflowed all over his face.

Joanna smiled broadly. It was like the warm, patient smile of a mother to a much-loved child who has just asked a silly question.

"Yes, Colin. I will," she assured him, laughing lightly. "Why do you think I came all the way over here?!"

Then she leant forward and kissed him.

Just as she had done with the red rose on the painful-parting platform.

Another deal was sealed.

31

THE CACTUS BLOSSOM

There was so much for an artist from a beautiful, bustling Polish city to discover in the heart of the beautiful, tranquil Northern Ireland countryside. The manifold marvels of Nature, the delicate handiwork of God, seemed to cry out for her attention at every turn.

The country way of life was totally different to anything she had ever yet experienced. And she had chosen an ideal environment in which to learn about it!

James and Elizabeth Tinsley and their other six sons had taken Joanna to their heart as soon as she had arrived at their farm on that eventful summer Sunday. It soon became evident that they all loved Joanna.

Colin had already taken her to his heart, in a very special way, nearly a year before. And it was patently obvious to everyone that he loved her too!

It was on a Saturday, almost two weeks after she had driven into their yard, that she had her introduction to a procedure which was a complete novelty to her but run of the mill stuff for the Tinsleys.

Just as they were finishing breakfast, Colin broke the news to her, almost apologetically. He was afraid in case she should be upset..

"I know we were hoping to go away for a run in the car sometime today, Jo," he said, "But I cannot really go anywhere until this cow calves. We have her in the barn. I thought she would have calved last night, but now

I am almost sure it will be this morning."

It didn't matter to Joanna when they went away. If she could see a cow calving that would be as good to her as a day out to Portrush.

To Colin it was just a nuisance, an inconvenience on his day off from his work in Marks & Spencer's Sprucefield store. To her it was an opportunity to witness yet another of the wonders of Nature.

"When the cow is ready to have her calf do you mind if I go up to the barn to see the birth?" she enquired, almost hesitantly, not quite sure if such events were classified as being 'strictly men only'.

"Not at all! No problem if you want to!" Colin replied. Nothing was ever a problem to him as far as Joanna was concerned.

Just over an hour later Colin came into the kitchen where his 'girl-friend' was sitting chatting to Derek and Matthew, two of his brothers. These younger men seemed to have an insatiable desire for information about her home country, and they appreciated the enthusiasm with which she described Poland, and Krakow in particular.

"It shouldn't be long now, Jo," he informed the waiting novice, during a break in her Polish report. "The bones have slipped."

'The bones have slipped!'

That sounded frighteningly painful to her and she was shocked that it didn't seem to be worrying the matter of fact Colin one bit!

"Come on, we will wait for her out in the barn," he invited. Having been eavesdropping on their conversations from the living-room, James Tinsley, senior, Colin's dad, called through, "If you don't mind I'll come too."

Although not wanting to intrude on their time together, James was always aware that these sons of his could do with a bit of fatherly advice from time to time. So he followed them out across the yard, pulling on his cap as he came.

Colin and his dad went in through the five-barred gate which closed off the end of the barn where the cow was enclosed. Joanna stood outside the gate. That was near enough for her. It was close enough to see, but not close enough to be involved.

The first thing Joanna saw was the cow, lying down on a pile of straw. And all she could see was cow. Big, black and white cow. A Friesian.

It wasn't long, though, until Colin called, "Look, Jo!"

When she did as instructed, Joanna saw what to her was an absolute miracle.

Two little white hoofs, completely identical, and sitting neatly side by side had begun to emerge. Close behind them came a little nose, lying between the two wet, skinny forelegs. Soon Joanna saw the head appear. Eyes, then ears.

She stood transfixed.

This was more awe-inspiring than any of the paintings in any of the art galleries she had even seen.

Then there seemed to be a pause in proceedings. The birth seemed to slow.

It was the shoulders. If the shoulders would come, the whole calf would soon come.

Perhaps she needed a little bit of assistance.

"A wee rope maybe?" James, who was supervising events in an easy relaxed manner, suggested. This was no one day wonder for him. This was every day work.

Joanna was even more astounded to see Colin take two short ropes and loop a noose at the end of them around each of the two delicate looking little legs and pull on them gently, but firmly.

Slowly, and then at the end, all of a rush, the complete calf appeared. Soaking wet and in a slosh of water.

It was fantastic.

Then something even more fantastic occurred. The mother cow turned around and licked it, and licked it, and licked it, until she had it dry!

Joanna stood open-mouthed in wonder.

She had seen new life appear.

Shortly after it was dry the new calf tried to stand up on tottery legs.

First time up it collapsed again, its legs just folding up like the legs of a drop-leaf table.

Next time up it stood for about ten seconds, staggered, and down it went again.

But it didn't give up.

Perhaps it knew it had a secret admirer, for third time up, it stayed up. Life for it had begun …

It was after lunch time before Colin and Joanna made it for the afternoon out. But Joanna didn't care, she had seen something which she would never forget.

That evening on returning home, she went to check on her calf, and having satisfied herself that it was remarkably stronger than when she had first seen it, she telephoned her dad back in Krakow, to tell him about her day. And about that week.

Her afternoon trip to Portrush wasn't the big talking point though.

It was the new calf.

Joanna was so excited about this new experience that she had difficulty describing it in Polish.

She had been speaking only English now for the past two weeks, and when she came to describe the highlight of her week in her native language she was confronted with a problem. She had never encountered the Polish verb for 'to calve'.

So her garbled description went something like, "I saw a wonderful thing this morning … it was a cow … a cow …. you know a cow … and the cow was having a baby … no the cow was not having a baby … no the cow was not having a baby cow … it was a having a calf …!"

Back in his flat in Krakow, Michael Maciantowicz had a puzzled look on his face. Whatever it was that Joanna had seen that morning, and he was sure it had something to do with a cow, it seemed to have made a lasting impression upon her. And there could be no doubt about it, she certainly sounded happy!

And if she was happy, he was happy.

Her happiness increased, too, as the weeks progressed.

Early July was hay-making time.

It gave Colin's two brothers Trevor and Edwin great pleasure to teach Joanna how to drive the Blue Fordson Major tractor, and particularly how to change the gears. And the pleasure it gave them could not compare with the pleasure driving around a twenty-four acre field with a hay-kicker on behind, tossing hay, gave Joanna.

Only for the fact that she was sure it would become lonely and cold in the middle of the night, Joanna felt she could stay in that field forever. For no matter in what direction she pointed the tractor, there was a beautiful view. Driving one way she looked down over the shimmering waters of Lough Neagh, and when she turned to go back in the opposite direction Divis Mountain stood out in stark relief against the sky.

The constant up, down and around of that field, for hours, with the view ahead and the sweet smell of the hay all around was a most enjoyable experience for a city-born artist.

On one of her hay-kicking tractor-driving days Colin's Aunt Isabel sent tea and tuna sandwiches out to the field. To Joanna, sitting with Trevor, Edwin and James the father, eating those sandwiches on a pile of hay at the head-rig of that big field on a warm sunny day was as close to perfection as earthly conditions could ever become. They could never be absolutely perfect until Colin came home from work, though, and that didn't happen until around five o'clock.

Joanna's anticipation of Colin coming home time became a joke amongst the family.

Around four-forty every afternoon Colin's dad would remark, with a mischievous twinkle in his eye, "Do you not think it is about time you took Meg for a walk, Jo?"

Meg was the family's pet springer spaniel, and Joanna had become attached to the lively animal. She became very interested in her daily exercise routine, too, when she discovered that if she took the dog for her walk at a specific moment in the afternoon she would arrive at their favourite bridge just as Colin was passing it on his way home!

By August the call of the brush returned to Joanna. The peace in her soul, and the delightful rural surroundings made her feel that she would like to visit some art galleries and even possibly paint some pictures.

One day as she was surveying the work in a gallery called One Oxford Street she began to discuss the exhibits with the proprietor, Mr. Ross Wilson.

As he was ever on the lookout for new talent, Ross was intrigued to learn that Joanna was an artist from Poland, on summer vacation in Northern Ireland.

"Would you have any samples or photographs of your work that I could have a look at?" he asked.

In response to his request Joanna showed him a copy of the catalogue of 'In Hundred Places ...' which she happened to have in her handbag.

As he flicked through that catalogue the gallery owner became visibly engrossed.

"I am planning a small exhibition for early next month," he offered, obviously impressed, "Would there be any chance of you having anything ready for that?"

It was an interesting challenge for Joanna and she liked interesting challenges.

It was also an interesting challenge for her kind hosts, the Tinsley family. They had never had an artist living with them before, and they were keen to create a makeshift 'studio' for her.

Colin and Isaac helped her clear all the dusty clutter from the middle of the floor of a disused hayloft to allow her a working space of about nine feet square below the cobweb-covered skylight. Isaac, who was eager to help Joanna in her artistic pursuits, cleaned the glass in the skylight to help let in the light, and mended the leak in it to help keep out the rain. And the artist was ready to work.

Saturdays were away with Colin on his day off and Sundays were church both morning and evening, and for the other five days of the week, during the month of August, Joanna painted. Until Meg-walking time!

At the beginning of the next month she had five paintings, two large and three small, finished and framed in time for the opening of the Exhibition on Thursday, 8th September. And the fact that she sold some of those paintings came as somewhat of a relief to her in another consideration which she kept persistently relegating to the back of her mind.

It was time to return to Poland.

Now she had the fare home, but how would she ever face the long lonely drive back across Europe?

The thought of it broke her heart. Leaving all these caring people who had treated her like a daughter or a sister. And driving off and leaving Colin just standing there? How was she ever going to do that?

Whether it was the pain of the prospect of such a parting or his natural Northern Ireland chivalry, or a combination of both that motivated him, Joanna didn't know, but she was thrilled at a proposition he put to her one day, down by the old stone bridge.

"In this country we have a tradition that if a boy has a date with a girl he takes her home. How would it do Jo, if I took two weeks holiday from work, and took you home?" was his suggestion.

Joanna stared back at him, her puzzled face a picture of both admiration and astonishment.

"You mean to Poland?" she asked, incredulously.

"Yes, I mean to Poland. I would like to leave you home," he affirmed.

So it was that in late September Colin and Joanna packed up the red Metro, said their farewells to the family, and set off on the three day drive across Europe.

And in all that time Colin never once wished he had fallen in love with a girl from nearer home. Somebody from Cookstown instead of Krakow. Never once.

He was so happy that God had led him to Joanna. For Joanna was a joy to be with. Anywhere.

On arriving back in her home city it was Joanna's tum to introduce Colin to her dad, Elizabeth, and younger brother Michael, the only three still at home.

They were pleased to meet this sincere lad from Northern Ireland who didn't speak a word of Polish, but they understood the language of love when he looked at Joanna.

In the living-room that evening Elizabeth said, "Look over there at that cactus, Joanna. Do you see the two blooms on it? We were amazed this morning to see it in bloom. That cactus has never bloomed for us before and I believe it is only supposed to bear one white flower, once every seven years. But this morning it had those two beautiful white blooms!"

Joanna was touched.

To her that was a sign. As well as being Colin's welcome to Poland, it was also another seal of their love, provided this time by their God and loving caring Heavenly Father, creator and sustainer of all things, including cactus plants.

Next morning the blooms were gone.

32

THE PIG'S TURKEY

If Dundrod was a new experience for Joanna, then Krakow was a new experience for Colin. Yes, he had been there before on a romantic weekend almost a year previously, but that had been as a tourist. Now he had arrived as a friend of a resident in which capacity he would have an opportunity to see much more of the city, and meet at least a few of its people.

On their first Sunday back in Poland Joanna took him to the Baptist Church where she had been shown such practical love and given such spiritual help in her early days as a Christian. They were both delighted to discover that the speaker that morning was an American missionary. So even though his native Northern Ireland seemed ever so far away, Colin was thrilled to hear the living Word of God read and taught, in English.

Those were two wonderful weeks. The carefree young couple often returned to the street cafe where they had first met, and shared their first impressions of each other, with each other. They strolled though the Kazimierz district, the old Jewish quarter of the city, or round the Planty, or up to the castle, or down by the river. Krakow had something different to offer for every day.

There again they hated to even entertain the thought that this time of total togetherness could ever end.

However, hate it or not, by the beginning of the second week Colin saw 'date of departure' looming up before him. He was scheduled to leave Poland on Friday afternoon. So Thursday would be his last night in Krakow. And unknown to Joanna he had been making secret preparations for that evening.

For four days, every time they had some time together, Michael junior had been teaching Colin some Polish. This wasn't Polish for pleasure though, this was Polish for a purpose. There was something Colin wanted to ask Joanna's dad before he left, something he need to have clear in his mind. A bit like the red rose deal and the girlfriend affirmation.

He needed to be sure about things.

If everything went according to his preconceived plan and he received the response he hoped for, it would always be a dream to cling to. A goal to anticipate. For it seemed as though it was going to be a long, long time before he would ever see his white lady again.

So Colin told Michael, junior, who had a working grasp of English, what it was that he wanted to say.

'Please sir,

'If the opportunity should arise could I have the hand of your daughter in marriage.'

It sounded ever so formal in English. It would sound less pompous in Polish.

That was provided Colin could get it right!

They worked hard at it, those two young men. Joanna's boyfriend and Joanna's brother. Late at night, early in the morning, or driving along in the car during the day, Colin practised his Polish.

"There are two mistakes you can make in this, Colin," his patient tutor told him. "The Polish words for 'please' and 'pig' are very alike. So, too are the words for 'daughter' and 'turkey'. 'Turka' is 'daughter'. 'Turki' is 'turkey'. Just be careful!"

Day and night Colin polished his Polish. He would be careful.

On that Thursday night, after what was to be their last meal together as a family for some time, Colin stood up and looked across at Michael, senior.

Joanna, the unwitting subject of Colin's speech to come, wondered what exactly was going on.

She didn't have long to wait.

With absolute gravity, and with all Michael junior's warnings ringing in his ears, Colin produced a crumpled piece of paper. He was determined that nothing was going to mar the magic of that moment.

What he hadn't considered, however, in all his periods of preparation was nervousness, which can cause hearts to thump, hands to shake, and minds to blank out completely.

Holding tightly on to the back of a chair with one shaking hand to steady himself, he held his scrap of paper in the other shaking hand.

Then he opened his dried up mouth. 'Pig sir,' he began.

Joanna looked across at him in amazement, not sure what was coming next. And not sure whether to laugh or cry.

Michael junior put his head in his hands and groaned, "Oh no!" Elizabeth, who was privy to the plan, burst out laughing.

And Joanna's dad, realising what kind of an ordeal this must be for the young man before him, sat looking encouragingly at him, arms folded, face unflinching.

Despite the mixed reaction all around him, Colin continued.

And did well until he came to the turka turki bit, and then he boobed again.

This time there was no restraint. Joanna, Elizabeth and Michael junior dissolved into hoots of laughter. Elizabeth rushed off to find a handkerchief to wipe the tears of laughter from her eyes, Joanna rolled around on the couch, almost in hysterics and on the occasions when he could control himself long enough to say anything, Michael junior repeated, "I told you! I told you! I told you!"

The amusement of the three who were chortling so uncontrollably stemmed not only from Colin's gaffes but also from the attitude of Joanna's dad.

The question he had just been asked was, 'Pig sir,

'If the opportunity should arise could I have the hand of your turkey in marriage?'

Yet he never flinched. Still the arms folded. Still the serious expression. Still the slowly nodding head.

Michael Maciantowicz was too much of a gentleman to offend anyone.

When Colin sat down again, returning his sweaty crumpled piece of paper to his pocket, the older man, assuming that the message was complete, and that there were no more clangers to come, gave his response.

Joanna's dad had no English, but was fluent in French, and so, presuming that this language would be understood by this likable lad who loved his daughter, said solemnly, "Absolument. Absolument."

Within fifteen minutes everyone had regained his or her composure, and everyone had a wonderful time of warm friendship. Colin in particular, felt satisfied

He had sealed another deal.

The 'pig' had agreed to let him have his 'turkey'. 'Absolument!' Next day was not so wonderful though.

Colin and Joanna sat holding hands in Warsaw airport, crying, barely speaking. They clung fiercely to each other, neither willing to let go.

Eventually Colin dragged himself away, showed his passport, and disappeared through the gate at immigration.

Joanna stood waving and waving, big tears running unchecked down her cheeks.

Colin turned and continued waving for as long as he could. He was still crying.

It was awful.

When would they ever meet again?

33

TWO WEDDINGS AND A GEARBOX

The winter days which followed the weeping in Warsaw were dark and lonely.

Joanna only felt like painting solemn scenes in sombre colours. The days for Colin seemed to drag.

They wrote to each other virtually every day and phoned each other often.

Occasionally the pair of love-sick twenty something year olds sent each other small samples of their daily life. They were simple everyday items but each had a particular and profound significance to a loving heart.

One morning, for instance, Joanna was surprised to receive a package from the postman. The attached customs declaration described the contents as being, 'One potato!' On opening it she found nothing but a scrubbed-up 'spud', in the perfect shape of a heart!

Other items to emanate from Northern Ireland were a small torch, 'to brighten up your day', a handful of straw, and some scented pine needles!

Joanna's offerings were more artistic. Her contributions to the I love you and I miss you but how can I express it? game consisted of a pen-line drawing of a cactus flower with two huge white blooms, sketches of the room where she was sitting, and faces depicting every sentiment known to man. From the pain of parting to the joy of meeting. And all stations in between.

The heartfelt nature of those letters showed the agony of the heartbreak the two young people experienced during those dark and dismal winter nights.

In an attempt to describe how she felt Joanna wrote once, 'I just felt I couldn't breathe normally. Couldn't take a full breath. Like I had just half of my heart. You have the other half. I had to stop my work for some time there, I felt so powerless...'

The one source of shared strength which sustained them during those difficult days of separation was their common Christian faith. Descriptions of sermons in church services, shared thoughts on scripture passages from private meditations, and prayers without ceasing for each other, helped to bind Colin and Joanna together in a unique way. For not only were they joined by a special human love but they were also united in the surpassing love of Christ.

Early in 1995 being apart had become almost unbearable.

So Colin decided he would have to do something to remedy the matter.

One Sunday afternoon in January he phoned Joanna.

After some loving, laughing preamble about the letters each had received from the other on the previous morning, Colin proceeded to the purpose of that particular call.

"I have a question to ask you, Jo," he began.

"And what's that, Colin?" Joanna countered, all bright and breezy, but having a sneaking suspicion of what was coming.

"Will you marry me?" he asked, his voice laden with love. There was a brief pause.

Joanna had expected this question to crop up sooner or later, the way things were going, so she was not caught unawares. She had her reply ready.

"Oh no, Colin. No. No, I can't. I can' ..." A deathly hush descended upon Dundrod.

That was, of course, only until Joanna went on to complete her response.

"I can't refuse! I can't say No!" Colin was ecstatic.

"Thank you, Jo! Thank you!" he exclaimed. Then he lowered his voice to add, "You had me scared there for a minute!"

"I was only pull'n' your leg!" Joanna giggled, having taken the opportunity to play a practical joke on the practical joker she had just consented to marry.

The prospect of becoming husband and wife had a settling, and in a different sense unsettling, effect, on both Colin and his bride-to-be.

They were thrilled at the prospect of spending the remainder of their lives together. That was the settling effect.

Having to wait until later in the year, until all the necessary arrangements could be made was a problem, though. That was the unsettling bit.

The telephone calls between Krakow and Dundrod increased dramatically both in length and in frequency over the next few months. For not only had the young couple their ever-deepening love to express, but on a more practical level they had also a wedding, involving two wedding services, to discuss. One in Northern Ireland for Colin's family, and one in Poland for Joanna's.

Initial and provisional plans were for a late spring wedding perhaps in May.

Joanna would make another three-day safari in her red Metro.

They would be married in Colin's church, then motor back to Krakow for a second ceremony in the Baptist Church there.

That was the plan. And everything was going well. Excitement had begun to mount. Colin and Joanna were counting off the days on calendars a thousand miles apart. Soon they would be together. Forever.

No bookings had been made but enquiries were well under way. Then came the hitch. More than a hitch, a hammer blow. Joanna had a calamity with her car.

Driving through the city one day she encountered roadworks. It was a resurfacing project and the road level had been lowered leaving the manhole covers sitting high. With traffic coming from the opposite direction so that she could not swerve to avoid one of the menacing looking covers, Joanna decided to drive over it, a wheel on either side.

Suddenly there was a rasping, sickening crunch. The car stopped.

Joanna went forward, and bending down to look below the engine she saw that the sump was stuck firmly on the manhole cover. Black oil oozed everywhere.

The gearbox was ruined. Transmission was gone.

The car could not be driven. It would have to be towed away. That night Joanna phoned Colin. She was in tears.

"Oh Colin, I have wrecked the gearbox of my car, and since it is a British car I cannot get a replacement here in Poland. What are we going to do?" she cried.

"Never worry, love," came her future husband's attempt at calming her down. "I should be able to pick up a gearbox for a Metro from a scrapyard over here somewhere."

"It's not the car I'm worried about!" Joanna went on to wail.

"It's the wedding!"

The wedding plans had to be postponed.

More waiting. More agony.

More planning, by letter and by telephone.

Eventually a date was set, and final preparations were made. In early summer, Joanna arrived at Belfast's International airport, suitcase in one hand and a suit bag, containing a white wedding dress with a magnificent Polish lace bodice and hemline, in the other.

After many weeks spent putting the final touches to earlier preparations, Colin and Joanna were married on Friday, 25th August 1995, in Lisburn Free Presbyterian Church, by Rev. Stanley Barnes.

What a blissful day that was! A day when two young people from different countries and different cultures whom God had called to Himself, and then brought together in a miraculous way, were bound together in the bonds of matrimony.

All Colin's family and many of the family friends attended the wedding and enjoyed the day. The wider family circle had all taken Joanna to their hearts, just as the immediate family had done, more than a year before.

The new Mr. and Mrs. Tinsley didn't have a lot of time to hang around though, to bask in the afterglow of 'their big day'.

In two days time they had to return to Krakow, to prepare for the Polish wedding.

They had fun when checking-in at the International Airport in Belfast on their way out.

"Are you travelling to Krakow on business?" an official enquired.

"No, we are going on honeymoon," Colin explained with a smile, for he was proud of his Joanna.

"On honeymoon?" the airline security officer was mystified.

"And what do you have in this banana box then?"

"It's a gearbox!" Colin went on, realising as he said it that it did sound somewhat ridiculous to be going on your honeymoon with a new bride and a second-hand gear box. So he proceeded to tell him the tale of The Metro and The Manhole.

Having inspected the contents of the banana box to satisfy himself that the story was correct, the security man looked at them as if to say, 'I have heard it all now,' and permitted them to proceed. To Krakow. And to wedding service number two.

Joanna had left the organisation of the Polish blessing on their marriage in Krakow Baptist Church on Saturday 2nd September, to the leaders of the church. They had assured her that they would arrange a fitting service for her, and they kept their promise.

She found it touching that the first hymn on their order of service was the one which had meant so much to her in her earlier days in that Church. And one which they had sung in English back in Lisburn on August 25th. Now it was her turn to sing 'Amazing Grace' in Polish once again. And she hadn't told anyone she wanted it!

Then dressed in her same wedding dress, and with Colin wearing a red rose in his lapel, his sign of a seal, a service of blessing was held. The organisers had kindly arranged for this to be conducted in English, to make Colin feel at home, with a translation into Polish for the benefit of almost everyone else.

All Joanna's family and many of her friends who were free and fit attended that ceremony and enjoyed it.

The warmth of the Christian love shared by the new husband and wife impressed many. Most of the guests were fascinated to hear Colin describe how they had first met in the street cafe in the Market Square, and how that they both believed that this was no mere chance meeting. He went on to explain how that they were both Christians and how he believed that God had brought them first of all to Him, and then together.

Theirs was a marriage solemnised in two countries, but organised long before, in heaven.

When the ceremony was over everyone moved on to the reception, and in keeping with Polish tradition all those coming to the reception brought flowers for the bride. Joanna was almost snowed under with beautiful bunches of all sorts of flowers in all shades of colour and most of them sweetly scented. Her brother Thomas was kept busy putting the flowers into temporary storage until they could all be properly arranged at some later stage.

Again in keeping with Polish tradition the reception lasted all through the night. The meal consisted of twelve courses, and between each course there were speeches and musical items. It was all so relaxed. So informal. Just as dawn was breaking outside it came Colin's turn to address the company in a short speech, which Thomas translated into Polish.

This he did with deep feeling referring to the guidance of God in his life, particularly over the previous two most eventful years.

The new husband summed up his feelings at the end when he told everyone, "I am looking forward to the future. With God's grace in my heart and my bride by my side I have nothing to fear."

He then turned to look down at his new wife, where she sat beside him, still radiant despite the long night of celebration.

"Look at her. Isn't she lovely?" he announced. "Krakow has lost a lady.

"And I have gained a wife.

"Poland has lost a princess.

"And Northern Ireland has gained a queen."

Everyone appreciated the warmth of his tone and the tears in his eyes. They knew he meant it.

34

WHAT COLOUR IS YOUR TOOTHBRUSH?

In the few days before the Polish leg of the wedding, Joanna's red Metro had been left into a garage in Krakow to have its well travelled gearbox fitted. This meant that when all the celebrations were over on Monday 4th September, and most of the wedding guests had returned to work, the newly-weds were free to embark upon their honeymoon proper, with the gearbox of the car actually in the car and not in a banana box!

For three blissful weeks they toured around Europe, driving through breath-taking scenery, visiting historic cities, and calling on some of Joanna's relatives and friends who had been unable to attend the wedding.

Later in the month, though, it was time for husband and wife to return and set up home in Northern Ireland, and for Colin to go back to work.

Having paid a final packing up and saying good bye visit to Krakow they set off for the Channel port of Calais, in France.

When they were directed to drive up the ramp on to the ferry Joanna feared another smashed sump saga. Their little car was so heavily laden with wedding presents, books, clothes and art materials that she was sure it was bound to catch on something, somewhere. To her great relief, it didn't.

The problem to come, however, was potentially much more serious than any problem they could ever have had with the car.

When passing through immigration control on Dover docks an official asked Joanna, "How long are you planning to remain in Britain?"

That question came as somewhat of a shock to the new Mrs. Tinsley.

"I am hoping to live in Northern Ireland," she replied, not sure how that would be accepted. "We have just been married in Poland and I am hoping to settle with Colin here, who is my new husband, in County Antrim."

"Do you have a permanent resident's visa?" the officer went on to enquire.

"No, I don't," Joanna was forced to admit. ""Do I need one?"

"Yes, I'm afraid you do," came the non too reassuring reply.

"You should have obtained one in Poland before you left. Pull over there and park," he continued, pointing to a vacant spot beside a brightly-lit building. "I will have to go in here and try to sort this out. There are a few places I will need to phone."

With that he disappeared into the building carrying Joanna's Polish passport.

As this conversation was taking place, Colin's heart had begun to sink.

What would happen if Joanna was refused entry to the United Kingdom?

What would he do if they told her that she would have to return to Krakow and apply for her visa from there?

When the immigration official had taken away Joanna's passport 'to try and sort this out', he found himself gazing across in stunned silence at his new wife. He didn't need to say anything.

The anguish on her face said it all.

After a few minutes she voiced both their concerns.

"What are we going to do, Colin?" she asked him, obviously wondering if she would be on her way back on the next boat.

'We can't do very much only pray," Colin replied. "Whatever decision they make we will have to abide by it."

That was fine for saying, but what if it would mean even a temporary separation?

So they did what Colin suggested was their best and only option. Sitting in an overloaded Metro on Dover docks as darkness began to fall and the increasing chill of an autumn evening began to creep in around them, Colin and Joanna prayed.

First audibly. Then silently.

At nine-thirty they were still sitting there. Praying, talking, hoping, waiting, praying. A security guard who had seen them sitting in the steaming-up car and understood their plight, brought them each a brimming full plastic beaker of hot tea. This was very welcome for before they drank it to warm their insides they used it to warm their freezing hands.

And still they waited.

They continued to pray and to talk, examining a series of 'what if?' options.

At one stage, frustrated with all the suspense, Colin exclaimed, "Jo, it says in the Bible, 'What God hath joined together let not man put asunder'! We believe that God has joined us together, so do you think He will let any man drive us apart?"

That was fine for saying, but did they really believe it? The wait was agonising.

Ten o'clock came and went.

Then half-past ten.

Colin and Joanna had already endured the anguish of two long heart-rending separations, one for nine months, and the other for almost a year.

But that was before they were married.

Could it happen again to a happily married couple?

Surely not. God wouldn't allow it. Or would He? Just to test their ….

At ten fifty-five their immigration officer reappeared. Without Joanna's passport.

"I have been on the telephone to both Poland and Belfast," he told the anxious pair, "and have decided to allow you to proceed to Northern Ireland."

That was marvellous! What an answer to prayer!

The officer hadn't finished what he had to say, though. And there was a 'but' in the next bit.

Addressing Joanna specifically, he continued, "But I am forwarding your passport on to our office in Belfast. You will both be called upon to attend there for an interview within the next month. If the authorities there are satisfied you will be granted a permanent visa. If not you may have to return to Poland and apply from your former home address."

Relieved that they would not have to be parted immediately at least, Colin and Joanna drove on to Northern Ireland where they set up their first home together in a cottage they had rented from Colin's cousin Gary, who had been part of that first, memorable, white-lady weekend in Krakow. The cottage had originally belonged to Colin's grandparents and was set in a picturesque location up in the rolling hills which bordered Belfast.

They were settling in happily and there was so much to tell the other Tinsleys about their second wedding and their honeymoon tour, and Colin was more than two weeks back at work, when the expected letter from the Belfast Immigration office arrived.

It was requesting Mr. and Mrs. Colin Tinsley to attend for interview on a certain date.

What would happen if Joanna was to be sent back to Poland now?

Surely nobody could be that cruel? Or could they …?

When the afternoon of the interview came Colin and Joanna attended as invited and were shown into separate rooms, where they were each interviewed by separate officers, both asking the same questions.

"How many brothers and sisters do you have?" was question one.

'I have six brothers and no sisters," replied Colin. "I have two brothers and no sisters," replied Joanna.

"How many brothers and sisters does your husband or wife have?" came question two.

"My wife has two brothers and no sisters," replied Colin.

"My husband has six brothers and no sisters," replied Joanna.

"Describe the view from the front window of your house," was another demand of both husband and wife.

"The front window of our house looks out over fields and hills. There are cows and sheep and dry stone walls. My Uncle Jim and Aunt Sue's farm is about three field-lengths away," was how Colin described it.

"We can see the farm owned by Colin's uncle and aunt. We are up in the hills and look out over fields all with dry stone walls. There are lots of cows and sheep in the fields," was how Joanna described it.

And so it went on. For almost half an hour.

One of the final questions put to both Colin and Joanna was, "And what colour is your toothbrush? "

"Red," replied Colin. "Red," replied Joanna.

"What colour is your husband or wife's toothbrush, then?" came the follow up question.

"Red," replied Colin. "We both use the same one and it's red." "Red," replied Joanna. "We both use the same one and it's red."

Soon the interview was over. All they had to do now was await the outcome, but having compared notes after the event both husband and wife were confident of a favourable result.

There would just have to be a favourable result. Anything else couldn't even be contemplated!

When the letter came a few days later Joanna was relieved to feel something which felt like her passport inside and when she opened the envelope she was delighted to discover her resident's visa.

So the immigration authorities had concluded that this Joanna Tinsley was not some illegal immigrant, but, as she had always maintained from the start, a happily married woman.

She was now free to live in Northern Ireland with her husband.

Forever.

God had answered their prayers.

And in this case what He had 'joined together' man had not even attempted to 'put asunder'.

35

PARDON ME, DO YOU SPEAK ENGLISH?

With all the uncertainties about immigration behind them, Colin and Joanna could settle into their little cottage in the hills. They were so happy together, both in their home and in their faith.

As she began to appreciate the magnitude of the challenge facing her, setting up a new home, adjusting to a new culture and communicating in a new language, Joanna leaned heavily upon two pillars of strength. Two sources of solace.

One was her love for Colin. The other her love for her Lord.

One morning, during her morning Bible study, and contemplating the days and years to come in the will of God, she wrote, in Polish, on the inside cover of her precious Polish Bible, a personal dedication.

It was both the prayer and the pledge of a full heart.

'Oh God, my Lord,
Let my steps follow your steps,
Let my heart beat with your heart.
Let my mind think with your thoughts.'
Joanna. 2-10-95

That was to be her simple motto from then on. Joanna was vowing to do what she could, and go where she had to, in order to fulfil what she understood to be God's will for her life.

A Polish national, living in Northern Ireland, had to be prepared to make the occasional mistake in learning the language in a local context, day after day. The odd slip of the tongue or misuse of a word usually went unnoticed or was graciously overlooked.

There were, however, in County Antrim, as in America, times when Joanna's use of a word or phrase caused either amusement, or alarm. Or both.

When Colin was around there was never a problem. For in the early days he accompanied his new wife to the local shops in the evenings or at the weekends, to acquaint her with the district, and he was able to help with the purchases.

As time passed, though, Joanna decided that it was about time she undertook the family shopping herself, and everyone had told her about the 'great bargains' and the 'lovely fresh fruit and fish' in Lisburn market.

So on the following Tuesday Joanna ventured forth on a shopping expedition, alone. To Lisburn, and the market.

It was true, too, what she had heard. The fresh produce looked very inviting.

She had always loved fish, and planning to experiment with a special treat for Colin on his return from work that evening she stood beside the fish stall until she was sure there was no one else other than the stall holder within earshot, before asking confidently, "Could I have a slice of your throat, please?"

The wee man eyed this prospective customer with suspicion. Then suddenly it dawned upon him. This young woman was obviously 'a foreigner', from her accent.

He grabbed at his throat in mock terror, before responding with a sly smile, "No, I would prefer not to cut my throat for you! But is it a piece of trout you want?"

'Oh I am so sorry!" Joanna exclaimed, realising her mistake.

"Yes. It is a piece of trout I want."

Then late in January of the following year Joanna slipped up again. And again it was to do with food. And eating.

Before their first happy Christmas together as husband and wife many of Colin and Joanna's friends had been extremely kind to them, showering them with gifts.

One of those presents, and one whose contents they very much enjoyed over the festive season, was a 'luxury Christmas hamper'.

The Christmas pudding, mince pies, shortbread, fruit juice and canned food of every kind were all very much appreciated by the young couple and their many callers, but still they could not eat it all over the Christmas period. There was just so much.

That January evening Joanna had opened a tin of cooked meat for their evening meal. As Colin tucked into it with relish he remarked, "That's lovely meat, Jo. Where did you get that?"

"You like it, Colin?" she asked before answering his question and revealing her secret, in all sincerity.

"We are still eating that hamster."

It was Colin's turn to appear thunderstruck. He imagined there wouldn't be that much meat on a boiled hamster, so reckoned he was safe enough. Unwilling to let the situation pass, however, without milking it for every ounce of fun, he slithered off the chair, rolled in pretended pain across the floor, and cried out in agonized tones, "Tell me you meant hamper, Jo! Tell me you meant hamper!"

There was another problem Joanna had with the language, too, at first, and that was with reading the scriptures. As she found it much quicker, and much more meaningful, initially, to read in her native language, she carried her Polish Bible with her to every church service, and when the text was announced she turned it up.

That was O.K. when the text was familiar. The Gospels she was good at, the Epistles were easy, and the Psalms and the Proverbs were no problem.

One Sunday morning the speaker announced that he would be reading from Haggai.

There was a longer than usual rustle of leaves as the congregation searched for 'the place'. When he had satisfied himself that most of his audience were ready, he began to read.

Joanna, though, was lost.

Nothing in her Bible looked even remotely like what the preacher had announced. So she flicked through the pages idly, hoping for inspiration. An elderly man beside her took pity on her. She must feel awful. With a finger in the correct place in his own Bible, he reached for Joanna's.

Someone would need to help her out.

He opened the Bible and peered at it. Something funny here he thought.

This is definitely not The Authorised Version!

Reaching around to the right-hand pocket of his jacket he pulled out a glasses case, opened it, and stuck a pair of half-frame spectacles on the end of his nose. Then holding the Bible up closer to his face, he had another look.

The glasses hadn't been a big help, however. It still all looked double-Dutch to him.

Then, in frustration he turned to Joanna, pushed the Polish Bible back in her direction, Whispering gruffly, "Here, I can't read that!"

As it so happened it didn't really matter, for the minister had finished his reading and started on his sermon!

So Joanna never found Haggai!

But she was travelling upward on the learning curve.

And she would find it next time.

36

WILL IT BE O.K. DO YOU THINK?

After their wedding, and as he and Joanna were settling into married life together, Colin became increasingly concerned that there should be more to life than going to work and coming home, going to work and coming home. He felt an overriding desire to be more effective in his life in some way. In some significant and spiritual way.

By that time Mr. and Mrs. Tinsley, junior, had moved from their temporary residence in the cottage in the hills to a modern mobile home which they had sited on property belonging to Colin's father. Since this accommodation was slightly more spacious than the cottage, Joanna had begun to consider returning to painting, as she had some time to spare when Colin was out at work. It was a possibility, but not yet a certainty.

They were, as they had been from the first day they met, extremely grateful to God that he had brought them together. And extremely thrilled to be together.

It was when reading a Bible verse about the marital bliss which was so much a part of their lives that Colin was challenged by the exhortation which followed it.

One day he turned to Ecclesiastes chapter nine to read verse nine, as he had done more than once before. He felt himself constantly attracted to that verse as it expressed so succinctly what he intended to do for the rest of his days, in the will of God.

It said:-

'Live joyfully with the wife whom thou lovest all the days of the life of thy vanity, which he hath given thee under the sun … for that is thy portion in this life, and in thy labour which thou takest under the sun'

As he read on to the succeeding verse Colin was struck by the command, and the sheer common sense of the command, it contained.

'Whatsoever thy hand findeth to do, do it with thy might; for there is no work, nor device, nor knowledge, nor wisdom, in the grave, whither thou goest', was its practical advice.

Immediately upon reading those words Colin's mind flashed back to a motto or maxim he had often heard quoted in church, and in fact he had heard it mentioned just the previous Sunday. He could never quite discover whether it was from a hymn, or a poem, or whether it just depended on its singular potency for its popularity.

It was:-

'Only one life, 'twill soon be past,
It's only what's done for Jesus will last.'

No matter where he went or what he did over the following few weeks, Colin couldn't escape the moment of that message. The world and everything in it, and human achievement and everything related to it, were both temporary and transient. He wanted to do something more worthwhile. Make an investment or two for eternity.

To complicate matters for him, however, just when he was beginning to contemplate such weighty issues he was promoted in his daily job. He had worked for many years for a well-known multiple store, and was upgraded to supervisor of the night shift.

This presented a problem. The enhanced salary offered with this promotion would allow Joanna and he to live more comfortably. It would be tempting to attempt to quell his intensifying inner convictions and settle for the easy option.

But he couldn't.

He became more and more concerned about people around him in the world, both at home and abroad who had either never heard the Gospel, or who had never responded to its message.

It the early summer of 1996 Colin decided that he would like to embark upon a course of full-time study to prepare himself for Christian service so he approached some senior ministers and the Board of The Whitefield College of the Bible for advice.

All those to whom he spoke gave him the same wise counsel. Appreciating his unmistakable zeal and desire to serve God, but taking into account the very practical consideration that he had just taken unto himself a young wife, for whom he was responsible, they advised him to wait for a year before giving up his secular employment to attend College. In that year he should pray diligently about the matter and discuss it at length with Joanna. He should also give careful consideration to which course it was he wanted to follow. The four year course leading into church ministry, or the two year course with an emphasis on missionary training.

The answer to that second question relating to choice of course was determined later that summer.

The young couple had gone to Spain for a camping holiday and one beautiful sunny morning Colin was lying outside their tent, engrossed in his daily Bible Reading.

It was then that he discovered a verse which he had never before even known existed in the scriptures. And it struck him as a bolt from the blue. As a clear indication from God.

The section Colin was reading that morning was the nineteenth chapter of the second book of Kings in the Old Testament, and it was the twenty-ninth verse which seemed to invite him to stop and read it again. And again.

To him it was so clear:-

'And this shall be a sign unto thee, Ye shall eat this year such things as grow of themselves, and in the second year that which springeth of the same; and in the third year sow ye, and reap, and plant vineyards and eat the fruits thereof.'

To the prospective Bible College student, the message of that verse was clear. Colin's interpretation of the verse was that things were to remain the same for two years, but in the third year he was to sow and reap. In other words he was to go to College for two years and in the third year commence putting his training into practice, by beginning to sow the living seed of the living Word of God. Start to preach the Gospel.

During the winter months Colin and Joanna often discussed the future. They were both interested in serving the Lord who meant so much to both of them. But there were practical matters to be considered. If 'the bread-winner' decided to leave his now reasonably well-paid job, what would they live on for the two years of the course? And apart from that, how were they going to raise the money to pay the College fees?

That made Joanna make up her mind.

She said to her husband one evening, "I will do a few paintings and try to have them included in an exhibition somewhere. If I could sell one or two it would help out with our expenses."

Colin was appreciative.

"That would be great, Jo," he enthused. "Will we be able to manage, though? Will it be O.K. do you think?"

If she had sneaking doubts she didn't dare let her husband know.

"I believe God has brought us together, and I believe it is God who has put the desire in your heart to serve Him. And I believe God will be able to see us through," Joanna assured him.

Late next spring Colin approached the shift manager of the store where he worked and asked to be stood down from his position as supervisor from September, as he was planning to go to Bible College.

He volunteered to work sixteen hours per week at nights or on a Saturday, if the company would agree.

The manager told him that she admired his dedication and was willing to grant him his request, but asked him to consider carefully if he was 'doing the right thing'.

Colin knew he was 'doing the right thing'. For he believed that what he was doing was God's 'thing'.

But there was a big drop in take-home pay from forty hours per week, and occasionally more, if there was overtime available, to sixteen. Could they possibly keep themselves, and Colin at Bible College, on that? Coupled, of course with the uncertainty of selling 'one or two' paintings 'now and again'?

Will it be O.K., do you think?

37

IT'S NO JOKE!

During that autumn Joanna set up a studio in their mobile home. If God was calling Colin to go to Bible College, He was also calling her to support him, both physically and spiritually, in every possible way.

Now she didn't feel the need to paint in muted mode.

Now she wanted to express, if she could, the light and love which surrounded her life.

The first painting she did was of harvest. A picture bathed in warmth and light.

Bales of straw lay dotted across rich golden fields. A road dissected the fields as it stretched off towards a small cluster of farm buildings which were suffused in a gentle light, glowing in from the horizon. This road was not completely smooth and flat and easy, though, but undulating. It went up, dipped down, then rose steadily upwards again.

The focal point of the painting was a solitary, simple cart, travelling towards the homestead in the distance. That was its goal at the end of its journey. A red triangle painted on the back of the cart pointed onward, and upward. In the direction of the light.

Since becoming a Christian, Joanna had been fascinated to read of another artist who said, "If I paint a landscape I like to paint the face of God hidden there."

That had become an aim of Joanna's when painting landscapes, too.

She sought to introduce the light of the glory of God into her work where possible. And in this latest picture which she entitled, 'Amish Road' the lone cart represented the journey of the saved soul. Onwards and upwards towards the source of eternal light.

There were no dominant blacks or dark blues in that picture. There didn't need to be. True enough, there were ups and downs. But even these were relieved by the light and warmth all around.

That was Joanna's story, in oils, yet again.

She had merely portrayed in that one picture all the basic shades of light, love, hope and peace which had subtly combined to become part of the complex panorama of her life, as a now-saved-and-satisfied soul.

Having completed 'Amish Road' Joanna then went on to paint a second, slightly smaller picture. This one was again on the theme of light, with street lights and car headlamps creating a crisscross pattern of light to dispel the gloom of a city street. This one she named 'Street Lights'.

In late January, 1997, Joanna submitted her two paintings to the Royal Hibernian Academy of Arts in Dublin. She was anxious to have them at least considered for the Academy's forthcoming annual exhibition.

Having sent in her work all she could do in the meantime was carry on painting something else. And wait, and wonder, and pray.

Early in March, when she was just beginning to resign herself to the fact that her paintings had been passed over for exhibition, she received a letter to inform her that they had been accepted. Both of her paintings would be hung in The Royal Hibernian Academy of Arts Exhibition, 1997, which was to be held from 22nd April until 17th May.

She could hardly wait until Colin arrived home from work that evening to tell him. How they both rejoiced and praised the Lord!

Perhaps now that the paintings were in the exhibition, someone might even buy one of them. That to them would be a sign that everything was going to be O.K.

Another wait. There was nothing they could do for a second time, however, except wait until April, until the exhibition opened. Until the paintings went on display.

How would they be received by the art critics? And General Public and his army. What would they think?

One bright, spring morning Joanna had gone out to the hen house to collect the eggs. Colin and she had started to keep a few hens to have some fresh eggs, and if there were any left over they could be sold. Anything that would help them save a few pounds would always be welcome.

Any time she left the mobile home she carried the cordless phone with her for Colin occasionally rang during his morning tea break.

She had almost reached the hen house when the phone rang. When she answered it Joanna was surprised to discover that it wasn't Colin, putting on a funny voice, and trying to pass off some crazy message.

It was, instead, a cultured lady's voice enquiring, "Is that Joanna Tinsley?"

Rather puzzled, and unsure at first whether on not to reveal her identity to a stranger, Joanna replied, hesitantly, "Yes. Why?"

"Well, if you are Joanna Tinsley I am ringing to inform you that you have won The Fergus O'Ryan Royal Hibernian Academy Memorial Award at our 1997 Exhibition,'" the voice continued.

Joanna laughed.

"You must be joking!" she exclaimed.

There was a pause at the other end. It was the turn of the caller to be taken aback. "I am not joking!" she assured the sceptical egg-collecting artist, when she spoke again. "This is serious. This is true. It's no joke!"

"I'm afraid I still don't believe you," Joanna persisted, not just quite as forcefully as before, but gently resolute, nonetheless. "Colin probably put you up to this!"

Another pause at the other end.

"And who is Colin?" the voice came back eventually.

"Colin is my husband," Joanna thought it best to explain. "And this is the kind of trick he plays on me all the time!"

The lady on the line was fast becoming exasperated.

"I'm telling you, this is no trick. And it's no joke. But if you like to, you should ring The Royal Academy and confirm it!" she replied.

"Thank you, and sorry to sound so awkward, but I think I just will," the still incredulous Joanna responded. "Good-bye and thank you, again."

And thus it was left.

Forgetting all about hens and their eggs, Joanna rushed back into their home, searched out the Dublin telephone number, and rang the Royal Hibernian Academy, as the bewildered caller had suggested.

This time she reached someone else in the office. After excusing themselves for a moment to consult the prize list they came back with the same message.

Yes. What the first lady had said was true and would be confirmed by letter within a few days.

Joanna could barely believe it, even after having it independently verified, and she determined not to tell anyone but Colin until the letter of confirmation arrived.

And it did, as promised, 'within a few days'.

The astounded artist was dumbfounded when she opened it and read:-

April 28, 1997

'Dear Joanna,

'The President, Council, and Members of the Academy are pleased to inform you that you have been selected as the winner of the Fergus O'Ryan RHA Memorial Award.

'I have pleasure in enclosing your cheque. Congratulations and all good wishes :'

And it was signed by the Administrative Secretary.

Colin was delighted to hear the news when he rang Joanna from work in his lunch hour. It seemed that God was beginning to show the young couple something. And that was only the starter.

The main course, and a whole variety of sweets were still to come.

After the Exhibition closed in Dublin, Joanna was contacted by a Member of the Academy and informed that although it was 'Street Lights' which had won the Award, her other painting, 'Amish Road' had been one of the main talking points of the entire Exhibition. So much so, indeed, that The Royal Academy had decided to purchase it for their permanent collection!

Joanna's personal expression of living in the light, and journeying home towards it, not as teenage searching pilgrim now, but as a mature and satisfied one, had been chosen to hang in the Royal Hibernian College of Arts in Dublin!

As a result of that award in that exhibition a steady trickle of people began to make enquiries about her work. Not all that many, and not loads of money. But there was an assurance that God could provide.

The lesson their bountiful Heavenly Father had chosen to teach his willing to be obedient children was that He was 'able to do exceeding abundantly above all that they could ask, or even think'!

And the art was the main course. The staple diet. If all else failed, they could live on it.

The variety of sweets, the course which left the most pleasant and permanent taste in the mouth, was the interest and practical help of many different Christians from many different backgrounds. When they heard that Colin was planning to go to Bible College they pledged themselves to help him.

The lesson had been learnt.

The question had been answered.

God had indicated that by His power and through His people they would be amply provided for.

Yes. It would be O.K.

38

THE GENTLE LILY FLOWER

Monday, April 28, 1997.

It was probably the ordinary beginning to another ordinary week for many, but it was a significant day in Joanna's life. For on that day, two things happened.

In Dublin the letter was being written, informing her that she had won an art award, and in Lisburn, Dr. Alan Cairns began five nights of Bible teaching in the Free Presbyterian Church.

Since coming to Northern Ireland, Joanna had begun to revel in the study of the scriptures, discovering new gems almost every time she opened her well-marked Polish Bible. This five-night session would afford her a precious opportunity to hear the Bible systematically expounded.

She didn't miss a night.

And she was not disappointed. On the contrary, she was delighted to delve into depths of truth she had only heard mentioned in passing, before. Night by night she was there with her Bible and notebook, waiting for the service to begin. She couldn't get enough of it!

Here there was, dwelling in one refined body, a once-darkened soul now surrounded by the Light of the World, a hungry soul craving ever bigger portions from the Bread of Life, and a thirsty soul in a permanent pant for Living Water.

Dr. Cairns took as his theme for the week, First Corinthians chapter one and verse thirty, from the New Testament.

" ...Christ Jesus, who of God is made unto us wisdom, and righteousness, and sanctification, and redemption.'

It was all so new to Joanna. She sat there night by night, her face aglow, drinking in the Word of God.

So many of the statements Dr. Cairns made reminded her of the contrast between her former life and her present position, that she wrote them down in the red notebook she carried with her. Then she was able to read them later, and highlight them for future meditation.

Simple statements, which many of the congregation would have heard before came to Joanna with the freshness of a spring morning.

Thoughts which meant to much to her, were methodically recorded in her book ...

'You do good things for God, because He first did great things for you.

'You don't do good things to get something for it, but because He first did something great for you.'

'God's pleasure should be our purpose in life. That's why we are here.'

'When God saves you He totally cleanses you and gives you Christ Himself as your wisdom. That means that from that point on you can think straight. You don't need to be afraid to think. You just look at everything in the light of the cross and call upon God to give you Christ as your wisdom.'

'Behind the flesh and blood there is a spiritual world with its spiritual battle.'

'True joy, real joy, can only be enjoyed by justified people.'

'Redemption is total, absolute, and permanent.'

'A healed soul, in a healed body, in a healed environment, that's redemption.'

What treasures of truth!

Joanna thought about them, and many more for weeks. She especially liked the concept of not being 'afraid to think' any more. That had been her position before her salvation. She had thought so much that she had almost become 'afraid to think' for fear of discovering some deeper dilemma than the one in which she currently found herself.

And she knew all about a spiritual world with spiritual battles, too. She had fought in the front-line of some of those battles!

What Joanna didn't know as she attended those meetings was that her very presence there with her obvious avid interest in the message, was an encouragement to the speaker. Dr. Cairns used to love seeing her leave those meetings, her face bright with the light of the glory of God.

How she had once longed to be like Martin, with his gentle grace and angel face. And now that goal had been achieved.

At least, that was how Dr. Cairns saw her. Like an angel. Her cheeks were shining, her eyes were sparkling. and her whole being radiated the reflected rays of the Sun of righteousness, Who had arisen in her heart, 'with healing in his wings'.

Later that year, in September, Colin began his studies in The Whitefield College of the Bible, Joanna continued to paint, and God continued to provide.

The young couple continued to be bound together in that love that united them to one another, and to God. And they became all the more convinced, also, that Colin's future lay in the service of God, in some capacity.

In January, 1998, with Colin busily engaged in his studies, and due to attend a special week of prayer, Joanna decided to pay a visit to her family and friends in her home city of Krakow.

Everyone was glad to see her when she arrived, but she missed her husband so much. So the letters began again. These were not crazy, passionate, say it with spuds and handfuls of hay dispatches now, though. There was evidence of a maturing love in the more recent epistles. The love hadn't gone away. It was still very much in evidence, only expressed rather differently.

One that thrilled Joanna's heart was the one Colin wrote to her, totally composed from verses of the Bible. It brought a tear to her eye to read:-

'Dear Joanna,

'John 16 v.16
'A little while, and ye shall not see me: and again, a little while, and ye shall see me, because I go to the Father.(in prayer for you)
'Psalm 40 vs. 1 & 5
'I waited patiently for the Lord; and he inclined unto me, and heard my cry.
'Many, O Lord my God, are thy wonderful works which thou hast done, and thy thoughts which are to us-ward; they cannot be reckoned up in order unto thee: if I would declare and speak of them, they are more than can be numbered.
'2 John v. 5
'And now I beseech thee, lady, not as though I wrote a new commandment unto thee but that which we had from the beginning, that we love one another.
'1 John 4 vs. 7-8
'Beloved, let us love one another: for love is of God; and every one that loveth is born of God, and knoweth God.
'He that loveth not knoweth not God; for God is love.
'2 John v.12
'Having many things to write unto you, I would not write with paper and ink: but I trust to come unto you, and speak face to face, that our joy may be full.
'3 John v.14
'But I trust I shall shortly see thee, and we shall speak face to face. Peace be to thee. Our friends salute thee. Greet the friends by name.

Colin.'

What a letter!
What an expression of heavenly love in earthly lives!
Joanna cherished that letter, carrying it about with her everywhere in her handbag. And it was to come in useful, to the point of actually proving spiritually profitable, later in her holiday ...
It was mid-afternoon in mid-January.
Krakow's market square was covered with well-trodden snow, and cosily-clad people hurried across it, more concerned about staying on their feet than studying the architecture. There was not a portrait painter,

colourful flower-seller or time-wasting tourist to be seen. Even the ever-present pigeons were all huddled together for heat, with feathers fluffed out, on the roof of the Cloth Hall, or high up on the Town Hall Tower.

This was winter.

Winter or no winter, though, Joanna wanted to make the most of every moment in her lovely city, and so she had been strolling across the frozen square when she heard a man's voice calling her, from off to the left.

"Joanna! Joanna! Can it possibly be Joanna?" came the astonished query.

Turning to face the direction of the call, the visitor saw a man, whom she did not immediately recognise in his winter wrap up gear.

"It is Joanna!" the stranger exclaimed. "Where have you been all this time? And what are you doing back in Krakow?"

"Marc!" Joanna replied, recognising him at last.

In her earlier, seeking, searching, dissatisfied days, Joanna had met Marc and talked things over with him often in the Buddhist canteen, for this friendly young man was a devout Buddhist.

As she began to explain that she was now married and living in Northern Ireland, Marc realised that this former friend had so many interesting tales to tell that he made a practical suggestion.

"I so much want to hear all your news, Joanna, but we are going to be frozen standing out here," he said, before going on to enquire, "Would you have time for a cup of coffee?"

When she said that she would, they settled themselves in one of the many cafes around the square, now all operating an inside-only policy, and the story began.

Marc sat mesmerised as Joanna told him of Colin, and how they had met, 'over there in that cafe at the corner', of their shared Christian faith, and of their wedding.

"In fact," Joanna went on to remark, "I received a letter from Colin, just yesterday, for my birthday. It is all in quotations from the Bible. Would you like to read it?"

"Yes, I would love to, if you don't mind. As long as it's not too personal!" Marc replied.

"No, it's nothing like that!" Joanna laughed, producing the letter from her handbag, and passing it across to him. She knew reading it would be no problem to Marc as he had lived for many years in America, and was fluent in English.

The expressions of wonder and admiration on his face were a study in themselves, as he read down the love letter from scripture.

When he had finished he folded the letter carefully, almost reverently, and returned it to its happy owner.

"That is beautiful, Joanna! It is almost like poetry!" Marc declared. "Did you say that was from the Bible?"

"Yes. That is from the Authorised Version of the Bible," came the reply. They talked on for almost an hour, with Joanna taking the opportunity to tell him how she had discovered peace and fulfillment in her faith, and how she loved reading the Bible. When she also showed him a small album of photographs of her paintings he studied them intently before remarking, "I can see a spiritual strength shining out from these pictures."

When it was almost time to leave, Marc summed up his discoveries of the biting winter afternoon.

"Joanna, you have changed completely from the restless, rebellious young woman I used to know. You are now like a gentle lily flower. So delicate, yet so strong," he told her. "Somehow I feel that when I go back home to my small golden Buddha it will seem so insignificant compared to the wealth and depth of the faith you have found."

There was silence for a few seconds. Joanna was touched. Obviously her declaration of faith had made a big impression on her former friend from the Buddhist canteen.

'I will pray for you, Marc," she told him, when she considered it appropriate to crash into the sacred silence.

"Thank you, Joanna," Marc replied, rising from the table and reaching for his coat. Then with a twinkle in his eye he went on to address Joanna with pretend sobriety, and yet his request was deadly serious.

"I beseech thee, lady, that shouldest procure for me a copy of the Authorised Version of the Bible. If thou couldest I wouldest be very grateful. God bless thee now!" was his petition.

"I will. I promise," Joanna assured him, with a smile. "I will buy you an Authorised Version of the Bible in English and send it to you as soon as I return home!"

And she did, too.

The 'gentle lily flower' sent him a Bible as soon as she returned to Northern Ireland, accompanied by a letter, and followed by much prayer.

It was a specific prayer that the seed of the living Word of God would germinate in his life, then grow and blossom until it brought forth the sweet fruit of salvation.

She continues to pray for that.

39

THE RAINBOW

Sending that Bible to Krakow, and praying earnestly for Marc, served to focus Colin and Joanna's minds on what they had begun to recognise as their singular most important purpose in life. They both wanted to be effective for the Lord.

Joanna had been able to express her faith in a very practical way through her painting. And Colin was busy with his studies at Bible College, preparing for Christian service.

What each of them desired, more than anything else, though, was to be enabled to point some soul to Christ. To them this would be the ultimate heavenly stamp of approval on their work and witness, if they could only see someone else rejoicing in the wonderful Saviour they had found. So they began to pray earnestly, both individually and in their daily shared prayer times, that God would use them, at some time, and in some way, to lead some person to faith in Him.

They realised, too, that there was no point in praying for God to use them, and then sitting in the house! So they became more and more involved in a variety of evangelical outreach activities.

Early in the summer of 1998 Colin was the invited speaker at a long weekend in the C.E.F. centre in County Donegal, and Joanna had been asked to lead the bedtime devotions with a group of girls.

One evening during the week, at the group prayer time, she asked the girls to specifically identify something they would like to pray for, and she would do the same. The girls requests were for a variety of things, but Joanna renewed her burden in prayer, publicly, that God would save a soul.

Next evening, after the supper-time talk, Jemma, one of the girls from Joanna's group declared that she 'would like to speak to somebody'.

Since Joanna had come to know her well she undertook to speak to Jemma, and discovered that the ten-year old child would like to be saved. Here was her challenge, and Joanna approached it prayerfully. As they sat down together, Joanna prayed briefly for Jemma, and for guidance, and then after having read some well known Bible verses explained to her as simply as she could, the way of salvation.

When she was sure that Jemma understood the truth she was attempting to put across, Joanna asked her to pray simply and accept Jesus into her heart and life to be her Saviour and friend.

After a few seconds of nervous hesitation, Jemma did that, softly and quietly.

What joy and delight!

Jemma had found eternal life.

And Joanna had been the signpost used by God to show her the way.

Later that summer, Colin was taking part in an outreach team in Ballymena, County Antrim, with a number of other students from the Whitefield College. They were visiting homes, distributing tracts, and conducting meetings, both for children and adults in the evenings.

Every morning before they set out they prayed for God's blessing and on Friday, September 4, Colin had prayed very definitely that God would lead him 'to some soul today'.

That afternoon he and Mark, another student, were visiting along a street in the town when they met some children coming home from school.

When they had offered the boys and girls an invitation to their meetings, one of the children asked, "What is this all about?"

That sort of question presented an open door to Colin and Mark who relished every opportunity to tell anyone what the Gospel was 'all about'. Standing there in the street on that pleasant afternoon they explained simply how that God loved them, that Christ had died for them, and He was now calling them to come to Him.

The children seemed in no hurry, and persisted in asking further questions. Mark and Colin were in no hurry either, and they continued to answer every question.

Fifteen minutes into the conversation, one boy asked, "And can I be saved now? I mean here?"

When he was assured that he could, Colin and Mark prayed for him, and he trusted Christ standing on the pavement. And within ten minutes a few of his friends had done so as well!

What rejoicing!

God had answered the teams' prayers of the morning, and Colin's prayer of months.

They had seen young souls saved, and before the pair of students left Ballymena to resume their studies at College, they left the children's names and addresses with the local Free Presbyterian minister who promised to keep in contact with them.

Some time later Colin and Joanna were to prove that their God could answer their prayers. In an entirely different context.

Again it was a Friday.

That morning Colin had prayed, as he always did, for God's guidance in leading them both throughout the day, and then he found himself constrained to pray very definitely for divine protection.

"God please watch over us this day. Put a hedge about us. Shut us in with Thee, bless us in all we would seek to do in Thy service and bring us safely home this evening," was the closing burden of his prayer.

In the evening of that same day, Colin was preparing to set out to help in the Youth Fellowship in Hillsborough Free Presbyterian Church. The sun had just begun to set and the glowing sky outside was very inviting to an artist who had been working in her studio for most of the day.

"I think I will take the dogs for a walk before it gets dark, Colin," she suggested.

"That's a good idea, Jo," Colin replied. "Make sure you have your key with you, though, for I will have to be on my way to Hillsborough before you are back."

When she had made sure she had her key in the pocket of her long red coat Joanna set off into the sunset evening, the dogs trotting, sometimes beside, sometimes behind her.

It was all so pleasant and peaceful.

Suddenly Joanna's leisurely stroll was interrupted. She had to spring into action.

Her Alsatian, with which there had never been a problem before, had dashed through a gate and was into a field of sheep.

Although she had never yet in her life seen a dog 'worrying' sheep, Joanna had heard Colin's parents and brothers talking about it, and she had no particular desire to witness it. Especially not with her own dog!

She ran madly after him down that large field, calling his name, as she plunged forward.

But to no avail. The dog ran on, and he was quicker than she was.

Then as she began to become breathless and slow down Joanna became conscious of a thundering noise coming towards her.

Within seconds of hearing the sound, something powerful pushed into Joanna's side. The force was irresistible, and pushed her to the ground. She lay there, motionless, her hands drawn up instinctively to protect her head. Hooves thundered over her, pounding her into the earth.

It was terrifying. Every part of her body seemed to be crushed by the weight of seemingly hundreds of huge, hard hooves.

When she realised what was happening Joanna thought she was going to die, and just whispered in panic, "Oh God! Please help!"

What she hadn't noticed, in her blind dash after the dog, was that as well as the sheep, there was a herd of cows in the field. They had been frightened by the running, barking dog, and the running, shouting woman, and had decided to do some running themselves.

Unfortunately for Joanna she was their target, their finishing post.

It was all over within a minute.

Dazed, she dared to look up.

The herd of cows had stopped at the other side of the field, and the dog which had been attracted to the sheep had abandoned his quest, and was coming towards her.

Carefully, cautiously she lifted herself up on to an elbow, and then when she thought the danger was past, at least for the moment, she stood up and grabbed the dog's collar, unable to believe that she didn't have a single broken bone after such an ordeal.

Without making any sudden movement, she crossed to the opposite side of the field from the herd of cows, and walked along the barbed wire fence until she was able to slide through a gate and into an adjoining field. The other dog, who had been watching proceedings from a distance, joined them, and soon Joanna and her two dogs were back home again.

They were back home again, but when Joanna put her hand in her pocket to take out the key to open the door, it wasn't there! It must have dropped out in the middle of the cow field. And she was not going back for it!

By that time it was almost dark but she knew that Colin had a spare key hidden somewhere, so by a combination of diligent searching and passionate praying she found it in the fourth place she tried.

The mirror in their mobile home was just inside the door, and Joanna stood before it, gazing at herself.

Her face was white, where it wasn't blotched with mud. Her hair was a tangled mat, cemented with mud.

Her long red coat was a sinister work of art, worked from top to bottom in a hoof-print pattern of mud.

Her arms and legs were black with bruises. And brown with mud.

Although she was still shaking from her shocking ordeal, Joanna praised the Lord as well. She could easily have been killed in that field, she knew, but God had answered the prayer of the morning. He had brought her home safely, despite the danger she had been in.

The realisation that the God in Whom she had trusted more than five years before had preserved her life in that situation, she found absolutely amazing.

When Colin came home and she told him the story, he was shocked.

His first reaction was to tell her something she already knew. "You could have been killed out there, Jo!" he exclaimed.

Later as they sat chatting Colin told his shaken but thankful wife what he had been speaking to the young people about in the Youth Fellowship. It was about the devil. "Satan is a real person, with a real mission," he had told them. "His aim is to try to prevent people from coming to Christ, and when he fails in that, then to test those who do ... And be warned, if the devil isn't attacking you he is probably attacking the closest person to you..."

Little did he know how true those words were!

On the Saturday just over two weeks after the crushed-by-the cows Friday night, Joanna was sitting in the mobile home looking out. There had been a shower and suddenly she spotted something beautiful.

"Oh Colin, come quickly to you see the rainbow!" she called, already on her way out the door.

Alerted by the sense of imminent excitement in her voice, her husband followed.

That rainbow that day was extremely bright, and it formed a perfect arc. As they walked away a bit and then looked back their little mobile home seemed to be nestling at the heart of it. It was surrounded in the most majestic light.

When they stopped to stand stock still, holding hands, Colin said, "You know, Jo, when God first put His rainbow on the earth it was as a seal of a promise to Noah. And come to think of it, that promise was a promise of preservation, for He said that He would never destroy the earth again with a flood. And it is a symbol of hope."

Those were precious moments gazing at that rainbow, together. For both Colin and Joanna had a lot for which they wanted to thank God. Together.

There was answered prayer for the salvation of souls.

Preservation in times of danger.

And plans for the future.

40

THE TANGLED LAMB

Spring is an invigorating season in the country.

And Joanna, when she had settled into her new abode, absolutely loved it.

Sown seed. Sprouting growth. Apple blossom.

The signs of renewed life were everywhere. It was all so encouraging. So positive. So potentially fruitful.

The lambs were one of the supreme joys for Joanna. Small and white, full of frolicking fun, they were dotted around dozens of fields.

During their second season in the mobile home the farmer from an adjoining farm asked Joanna if she would like to foster three orphan lambs. Their mothers had rejected them, or died, and so the lambs would have to be hand-fed.

To a city-girl the call and challenge of this proved irresistible. Actually coming so close to these cuddly little creatures to be able to feed them! To play mother to them! It sounded wonderful!

Her lambs were just about a week old when the farmer brought them round to her, bleating balls of white wool.

Colin's dad, who had a lifetime's experience of farm animals, provided her with a specially-shaped feeding bucket for her charges. And a sucking-bottle, too.

Feeds, she was told, had to be given every four hours initially, both day and night!

For the first few weeks the three lambs stayed in a barn beside their home. Joanna was always thrilled to witness the tremor of excitement with which they greeted her every time she entered that barn with their bottle or their bucket.

They knew they could depend on her. She was more than just their food supply. Her presence brought them solace. They knew she cared for them. Joanna was both happy in, and in a certain sense humbled by, their implicit trust.

Just after Easter, her dad-in-law reckoned that Joanna's lambs were well enough advanced to be released into the luscious growth of the springing-green field beside their mobile. And how the lambs enjoyed that. After they were first granted the freedom of the field Joanna idled away much precious painting time just gazing out at them. She could see three-quarters of their grassy playground from her windows, and it gave her a quiet sense of satisfaction to watch them frisking around together, and then flopping down in a group when they had exhausted themselves with their exertions.

It was great to observe them continuing to grow.

Then one morning when Colin was away at College, and she was busy painting, Joanna heard a cry. It sounded like a baby or a young child at first, so she took no notice.

Sometimes the grandchildren visited at the neighbouring farm. And sometimes the grandchildren fell and hurt themselves, or fought and hurt each other, when they visited at the neighbouring farm.

It was probably the grandchildren. So Joanna went on painting.

Then the cry came again, loud and lingering. A piercing cry of pain. It sounded now as though it was coming from closer than the farm.

She cleaned the brush she was using, wiped her hands, opened the door, stuck her head out, and listened.

By that time, though, the crying had stopped.

Whatever it was, it seemed to be over. Perhaps the farmer had sorted it out.

And Joanna went back to her painting.

Within fifteen minutes the crying had recommenced. More plaintive than ever. It was heart-rending. Somebody, or something, was in trouble.

Joanna decided that it was time for action. She could do nothing no longer.

Pulling on her Wellington boots which had been Colin's first Christmas present to her after they were married, a kind of a welcome-to-Northern-Ireland present, she went outside.

The wailing became ever more pathetic, wafting on the gentle wind.

When outside, however, she was able to locate the cry. It was coming from the quarter of the field which was not visible from her window. Up close to the top hedge.

Only two of her three lambs were cropping at the lush grass.

And it was the third which was doing the crying.

As she drew closer to the source of the noise she realised one of the lambs had been caught somehow. It appeared to be struggling to get free.

Involuntarily she broke into a run.

On reaching the spot where the lamb was caught Joanna began to understand what had happened. A length of rusty wire had been discarded, after some fencing operation, up in the comer of that field. Grass had grown over much of it so that it was concealed from view. Obviously the lamb had been tempted by the long juicy grass around, had ventured too close, and had become totally entangled. In a frantic attempt to free itself the lamb had struggled wildly, and rather than helping its condition that made it worse.

Now the lamb was so tangled it couldn't even move. Its only hope was to cry out for help.

And help had heard and was now at hand.

Joanna spoke to it soothingly, and the bleating stopped. The lamb knew at once that if anything could be done to help it, this was the person to do it.

Kneeling down beside the frightened creature Joanna was able to establish the extent of its plight. The lamb's woolly coat was firmly enmeshed in the wire. Large chunks of wool lay around, affording a stark reminder of a prolonged, pointless struggle.

When she reached over to free it from the first fearsome strand of wire, the lamb crouched down silently, submissive. It seemed to know that the disentanglement process had begun.

It was painstaking, and occasionally painful work. A few undetected barbs of wire tore at her hands, leaving them covered in jagged scratches, as she laboured in love, to extricate the lamb from its wiry prison, a strand at a time.

Eventually it was free.

The tangled lamb wasn't tangled any more. Joanna had removed all the ensnaring wire and thrown it to the side.

The amazing thing was that for the first few seconds the lamb didn't even know it was free! Still it sat, submissive, subjecting itself to the gentle, liberating hands.

So the hands that had so kindly and carefully effected its freedom performed a further function.

Conscious of the pain it must have endured, and the terror which had been in its heart, Joanna used her now bleeding hands to give the once-tangled lamb a gentle push.

Slowly, shakily, it stood up ...

Then it took a few exploratory steps forward ...

Suddenly it bounded away, skipping, gambolling down the field, to join the other two, wisps of wool flying out in its wake!

Joanna stared, almost vacantly, after it.

Her mind was far away. She had returned, in thought, to Krakow.

She had once been like the tangled lamb. Totally surrounded by darkness and entrapped by evil. And the more she had struggled to attempt to free herself, the worse things had become.

Eventually, in the throes of misery, pain and frustration, she had cried, "God, if You are really there : Please speak to me."

And He had. He had heard her cry. He had come to her. And when she had submitted herself into His hands He had set her free.

Like the lamb, too, she hadn't appreciated the richness of her freedom at first. But when God, through His Word, His people, and particularly her husband, had applied a systematic series of gentle shoves, she was now, like the healed cripple at the Beautiful gate of the temple, in the Bible, spiritually 'walking and leaping and praising God'.

When reality took over from reverie again, and she was sure that she was not needed in the field any more, Joanna returned to the mobile home, kicked off her Wellingtons, and went in.

Another verse kept recurring in her mind. It was one from a story she had heard Colin use as an illustration a few weeks before, and one which she thought summarised her entire experience with God.

It contained the comforting words of Jesus to the woman who had been healed by merely touching the hem of His garment, when He assured her, 'Daughter, be of good comfort: thy faith hath made thee whole; go in peace.'

Joanna climbed up onto the couch on her knees, and looked out the window. She wanted another look at the tangled lamb. It was now perfectly happy and free, feeding with the others.

Then she looked down at the mess of her hands. They were streaked with her own blood from the rusty barbed wire. Red-black scabs had already begun to form over some of the deeper scratches.

Tears glistened on her cheeks as the spring sunlight streamed in on her face.

"Thank You, God!" she croaked, hoarsely. "Thank You!"

EPILOGUE

What happened since the year 2000 when the book was first published? Let me tell you. Ever since I was a young girl, I always wanted to travel. Looking back upon my life now, it is amazing how God has given me so many opportunities to do this. After Colin finished Bible College we have literally travelled the world sharing God's Word and the love of Christ with so many people, especially children. I had a privilege to paint in many of those places.

Colin didn't really know what his calling was in life when he went to college but he knew he must prepare himself for what was to come.

In the meantime I just continued to paint as I just loved painting. I worked with a gallery in Dublin and another one in Hollywood in Northern Ireland and I was in my element! Colin built me a nice studio and he always made sure I had what I wanted and was always there for me when I needed him.

He realised I had left my family and everything I ever had in Poland and the only reason I was living in Northern Ireland was because of love. Married life was so much fun, we did everything together and were always best friends, and that even continues today.

Sometimes people ask me: "How long did we go on honeymoon for?" I just tell them, "I'm not sure because it's not over yet!"

Colin is the type of man who is always on the go, his mind is always buzzing with ideas and he is so energetic. He amazes me at his energy as he never seems to be tired. This is always very infectious!

After Colin finished college we went together to the CEF training campus in Switzerland for the summer. It was here that the Lord burned the desire and burden for evangelising children into Colin's heart.

During the course I set up a studio in the attic of the CEF house. After completing the most important and vital parts of the course I was able to paint there. It was very soothing to paint in that place while listening to the cow and sheep bells ringing all day long!

I was preparing for next big exhibition back in Belfast which was to be held at the Wellington Park Hotel on Malone Road in Belfast in December 2000.

Upon completing this course and after a successful exhibition we were sent by the church to Jamaica for one year to pastor a little church. We absolutely loved this country. The people were so friendly and nice. Not only was Colin looking after the church and driving the church minibus nine hours on a Sunday but every day he wanted to go to schools to teach the Bible to the children. He even went early to race and play cricket with the kids. He ended up going to 52 schools in Jamaica. We loved it!

I gave up painting for that whole year to help Colin and go with him to schools and be part of that whole work. It was a big learning experience for both of us. Pastoring and teaching the Bible several times a week was good training for Colin. Before Jamaica, Colin assisted the Rev Stanley Barnes in the Hillsborough church and after Jamaica his own minister, Rev Thomas Martin, asked Colin to assist him in his own church for a year helping with the youth and visitation etc. Then we were asked to go to Lock in South Australia for two years, this was a farming community. Colin didn't take long to make decisions; he was ready to go when he was asked. Our lives were now in God's hands, He knew best for us and we were both very excited.

Again Colin pastored a small country church for two years. We absolutely loved that, Colin was in his element living amongst the farming community and I could continue to paint.

One of the things that inspired me to paint in Australia were children's beach missions we organised there. I painted several children's portraits, one of them called 'Fashion Show' (attached photos). Since we lived in a farming community I painted a few paintings with 'A Harvest' theme. I also took part in the Adelaide Festival of Arts in the year 2004. To my big surprise all the paintings I exhibited there were purchased by a big Australian art collector!

After two years were up instead of returning home we decided to buy a camper van and spend another year travelling to Perth, Alice Springs, then on to Darwin, right across to Cairns and the whole way down the East coast to Melbourne and across to Tasmania.

During this trip Colin visited and spoke in 100 schools, reaching and speaking to thousands of children and young people. He just loved doing this and I was so happy just to be there to help him in whatever way I could. I was able to paint once we arrived and settled in Tasmania for a while.

Our time in Australia inspired me to paint such paintings as 'Lady with umbrella', 'Self portrait as an Amish girl' and many others.

After returning to Northern Ireland I felt I needed a studio at our new house in Kinallen in County Down. One day we were standing in the garage of our house and I just said without even thinking: "This could be a great studio..." A couple of weeks later a builder turned up in the morning to start the work. That was organised by Colin!

In May 2007 Colin established and launched his own ministry called "Hope for Youth Ministries." This was a name that would be used to develop what was to become a very busy ministry.

At this time Colin joined a team from Coleraine University to go to Poland to do a Christian camp with Henryk, a Polish missionary. Henryk asked Colin if he knew anyone who could teach the Bible to the Polish children. I remember Colin smiling and saying: "I not only know someone but I have a translator as well!"

Looking back now with Colin we have taken 30 teams, hundreds of volunteers to Poland to do camps, reaching the Polish children with the gospel, the majority of them from orphanages and disadvantaged backgrounds. This is a major part of our ministry and we love it. I get to reach my own people with the gospel, the gospel which changed my life.

That same year I prepared a major solo exhibition. It was to be opened by The Minister of Arts Edwin Poots and Lord Mayor of Lisburn James Tinsley. It was to be a big show in a new gallery in Belfast. The day before the show I answered the phone and it was my brother Thomas phoning from Poland and asking about the exhibition. At the same time the door bell rang so I opened the door and who was there .... my brother Thomas and his wife Margaret. That was a special surprise and Colin had something to do with it! Colin and I love to surprise each other from time to time and this was one of them!

Hope for Youth Ministry is an official charity and a full time ministry. We stepped out by faith many years now and the Lord continues to provide our every need. That means organising Bible clubs at home, speaking in over 400 schools in Northern Ireland and international mission trips abroad taking teams to many parts of the world. We have participated in and taken teams to Poland, South Africa, Kenya, Spain, Vanuatu, Hong Kong, China, Laos, Vietnam, The Philippines, Israel, Lithuania, Isle of Man, and are planning India, Nepal and Canada at the moment. Tollymore Forest continues to be the home of our annual summer camps in Northern Ireland.

The majority of our work at home in Northern Ireland is organising Bible fun weeks, mainly in public schools. It amazes me how Colin can do so many of these every year! Lately it increased to over 100. The Lord has blessed him with unusual strength and stamina. I love to look after him to make sure he remains fit and focused.

Unfortunately we were unable to have any children, although many times I was able to conceive I wasn't able to carry it through. God gave us the courage to understand and accept His will in this matter and now I treat Colin as my little boy and continue to look after him.

As we see how God can use us to reach so many children then we have to smile and agree that God's way and will is absolutely perfect. As they say in Philippines: God is good all the time and all the time God is good!

Our greatest joy however is to see children and young people come and put their trust in the Lord Jesus Christ. Over the years we have had the tremendous joy of seeing, counselling and leading hundreds of children to Christ. Colin has been able to write books for children, 17 to date, to help and encourage them in their walk with God. We use these as prizes in this work.

To finish with, what amazes me in Northern Ireland is all the friends and volunteers who have supported and encouraged us so much along the way. We have met and continue to be friends with so many wonderful, kind and caring people.

Thank you for your love, support and friendship. God continues to keep us on the road and He uses wonderful people to make this possible. Colin often says, "We do what we love because we love what we do", and it's so true!

I also love painting and expressing in my art work the joy and contentment that God has given me in life. I love showing through painting the tender protection, love and God's strength that I experienced in my own life.

Joanna Tinsley … the happiest wee Polish girl in Northern Ireland.
December 2013